ON GEOPOLITICS

ON POLITICS
L. Sandy Maisel, Series Editor

On Politics is a series of short reflections by major scholars on key subfields within political science. Books in the series are personal and practical as well as informed by years of scholarship and deliberation. General readers who want a considered overview of a field as well as students who need a launching platform for new research will find these books a good place to start. Designed for personal libraries as well as student backpacks, these smart books are small format, easy reading, aesthetically pleasing, and affordable.

Titles in the Series
On Foreign Policy, Alexander L. George
On Ordinary Heroes and American Democracy, Gerald M. Pomper
On the Presidency, Thomas E. Cronin
On Legislatures, Gerhard Loewenberg
On Environmental Governance, Oran R. Young
On Geopolitics, Harvey Starr
On the Supreme Court, Louis Fisher

HARVEY STARR

ON GEOPOLITICS
Space, Place, and International Relations

Paradigm Publishers
Boulder • London

Maps to accompany the text can be seen at the book website:
http://www.paradigmpublishers.com/Books/BookDetail.aspx?product
ID=356911

Copyright © 2013 by Paradigm Publishers

Published in the United States by Paradigm Publishers, 5589 Arapahoe Avenue, Boulder, CO 80303 USA.

Paradigm Publishers is the trade name of Birkenkamp & Company, LLC, Dean Birkenkamp, President and Publisher.

Library of Congress Cataloging-in-Publication Data

Starr, Harvey.
  On geopolitics : space, place, and international relations / Harvey Starr.
      p. cm. — (On politics)
  Includes bibliographical references and index.
  ISBN 978-1-59451-877-5 (pbk. : alk. paper)
  1. Geopolitics. 2. International relations. 3. World politics. I. Title.
JC319.S73 2013
327.101—dc23

                                                                2012041696

Printed and bound in the United States of America on acid-free paper that meets the standards of the American National Standard for Permanence of Paper for Printed Library Materials.

17 16 15 14 13   1 2 3 4 5

CONTENTS

LIST OF TABLES AND FIGURES

PREFACE

This book draws from work I have done over almost four decades of research and writing, and provides a synthesis of basic research suitable for students at a variety of levels. My hope is to offer an overview of several fields—geography, international relations, and conflict analysis chief among them—and to show how they interrelate. The relationship between geopolitics and international relations across the years has been one of alternating centrality and neglect. I try in this book to show how the current relationship is built on a view of geographical and spatial "possibilism" as well as multiple versions of "space." These approaches have resurrected interest in geography and geopolitics, and rescued them from the determinist and ideological dungeon to which they had been consigned since World War II. In this book I stress the importance of the spatial context for understanding international relations, highlighting the need to take both time and space into account, as well as both a locational view and the perceptual/symbolic/constructed view of space and place. By situating my discussion within an increasingly globalized, interdependent, and transnational world system, I also demonstrate how the relationship between geopolitics and international relations covers state and non-state actors alike.

CHAPTER 1
GEOGRAPHY AND INTERNATIONAL RELATIONS

Basic Assumptions and Interests

The study of international relations (or international politics, or world politics) sits at the convergence of human inquiry that crosses both time and space. In terms of time, analysts fall back on the *seeming* simplicity of locating events and explanations in the past, the present, or the future. Without such apparently simple categories, spatial or geographic elements have not been as frequently used to locate analysis. Yet, as geographers are always willing to tell us, no matter where you go, there you *are.*

Geography is inextricably intertwined with the study of international relations as one of the two primary components to the context within which events and explanations occur (and let's be sure to throw in description, understanding, and prediction as well!): time and space. For example, Anthony Giddens (1984, 132) argues that contextuality involves the notion that, "All social life occurs in, and is constituted by, intersections of presence and absence in the 'fading away' of time and the 'shading off of space.'" And theory, which drives our questions, our research designs, and the nature of our inquiry, must take context into account—with the utility and applicability of all theory being conditional.[1] Geography is also inextricably intertwined with the multi-disciplinarity required to study international relations, as well as with scholars' need to *cross boundaries* in order to do so. These are the key themes upon which this book rests.

I think it is important to begin with two (hopefully non-controversial) considerations. The first is that the substance and study of international relations are concerned with the basic questions of politics in the sense of Harold Lasswell's famous definition: "who gets what, when and how." That is, we are concerned with authority and power, in both their institutionalized and informal structures and processes, and their variety of outcomes and consequences for states and non-state international actors alike. To deal with this definition without the geographic or spatial context would be grossly incomplete. This book will address a number of the ways in which international relations may be joined to geography, both theoretically and empirically.

The second observation is that the study of international relations is, by nature, a multidisciplinary enterprise. As students of international relations range across levels of analysis (from the global system to the idiosyncrasies of individuals) and a complex of issue areas and problems, they encounter the phenomena and foci of many academic disciplines. Indeed, many current approaches to the analysis of international politics, in the words of Bear Braumoeller, reflect "theories that posit complex causation, or multiple causal paths" (2003, 209). Our concern with multi-disciplinarity and geography may be approached using Davis Bobrow's (1972,

4) two imaginary visits to the international relations (IR) section of a library. Even in a 1946 visit, the IR collection would cover several disciplines, composed of materials from political science, history, and law. Although the same disciplines are also represented in Bobrow's 1972 trip, he finds a number of fields have been added: economics, psychology, sociology, organizational behavior, cybernetics, operations research, systems analysis, and general systems theory. Note that a striking omission from both libraries is *geography*. In a pioneering piece on the relevance of the behavioral sciences to the study of international relations, J. David Singer (1961) discussed the need to give attention to the potential impact on international relations theory of anthropology, psychology, and sociology. Although students of international relations were to benefit from the findings, concepts, and methods of these disciplines, once again geography was not included.

What might account for these omissions? The contributions of geography and the role of geopolitics in the study of international relations were thrown into disrepute as a consequence of some of the nineteenth-century and early-twentieth-century geopolitical approaches having "promoted a very explicit ideological message, with a rather heavy load of pseudo-scientific dross," as well as having been reductionist and determinist (Østerud 1988, 198). The content of German "Geopolitik," based primarily on the Haushofer school, was perceived as a central component of Nazi ideology and contributed to a general questioning of geopolitical theory. The ideological component was related, in part, to the strongly deterministic nature of many geopolitical approaches. However, a "new geography," which developed in the last decades of the twentieth century, set out to be strictly anti-determinist, instead treating geography as one essential part of the context of possibilities and constraints that face foreign policy decision makers. Pioneers in this approach were the international relations scholars, Harold and Margaret Sprout, who characterized environmental determinism as follows:

> In practice, strict environmental determinism has generally referred to the thesis that some set of environmental factors, less than the total milieu, is sufficient to account for ... both the psychological behavior of human beings and the empirical outcomes of their undertakings. Applied rigorously, this philosophical posture envisages man as a sort of chip in the stream of history. He is borne along by a current which he is incapable of resisting, within a channel from which he cannot escape. (1965, 48)

From many examples provided in the Sprouts' various writings, two provide the flavor of determinist thinking. Richard von Kuhlmann, a German diplomat, is quoted as follows:

> geographical position and historical development are so largely determining factors of foreign policy that, regardless of the kaleidoscopic change of contemporary events, and no matter what form of government has been instituted or what political party may be in power, the foreign policy of a country has a natural tendency to return again and again to the same general and fundamental alignment. (Sprout and Sprout 1969, 41)

More starkly, the French historian-geographer Edmond Demolins, was cited (Sprout and Sprout 1971, 268) as observing that "if the history of mankind began again and the present surface of the earth were unchanged, that history would be repeated in its essential design."

The resurgence of interest in geography and spatial approaches to international relations over the past several decades has been based on a conception of geography that has replaced determinism with "possibilism," as clearly represented in the work of the Sprouts and in my own agent-structure framework of "opportunity and willingness" (Starr 1978). The possibilism of the Sprouts has been the basis for my development of the opportunity-willingness framework. I join with geographers in arguing that geography does not necessarily have a distinctive subject matter, but rather is a perspective on how context affects behavior. Based on my past work, I will argue that the context-behavior mode of thinking—linking micro-phenomena to macro-contexts—best joins political and geographic perspectives (see also Flint 2012).

A Personal Journey across Time and Space

Much of my own work has addressed questions that fit within this broad geopolitical perspective. Beginning with the development of the opportunity and willingness framework, I have engaged in collaborative research that has sought both to refine agency (willingness) and structure (opportunity) as well as to specify the relationships between them. Opportunity and willingness have also been clarified through efforts to operationalize them in the study of international relations. These investigations include the study of the diffusion of international phenomena, especially violent conflict, but also the spread of democracy and spatial aspects of cooperation. Undoubtedly, the central feature of my work has been a focus on the nature and effects of spatial proximity as operationalized by international borders.

Thus, I have a long-standing interest in combining opportunity and willingness, context, spatiality, and geopolitics. It would be useful, then, to provide a brief account of my own journey across *time* to get to where I am today (this *place*). Taking the title of the well-known book by geographers John Agnew and James Duncan (1989) *The Power of Place* literally, we need to start in New Haven from 1967 to 1971 where I went to graduate school. At one point Bruce Russett exhorted Yale graduate students to attend a presentation by Walter Isard, the founder of what is now the Peace Science Society (International), and whose articles we had read, and meet him afterward. Isard was trained as an economist and became the founder of the field of "regional science," incorporating geography and location theory with economics and economic development (see Boyce and Miller 2011). I had come to graduate school with a strong background in history (and thus a proper respect for the temporal context). As part of my graduate course work I had taken an international relations theory course from Russett, where I was introduced to the work of Harold and Margaret Sprout. Through their concept of the "ecological triad" (entity, environment, and the entity-environment relationship) their work sensitized me to the need to contextualize behavior and to be concerned with *how* the context or "*milieu*" (to use the Sproutian term) was linked to the environed entity.

Within this background (or context!), Walter Isard's discussion of regional science, with its *geoeconomics* focus, resonated even more sharply with me. Whereas my dissertation research on war coalitions stressed the temporal context, one of the key dependent variables was the loss or gain of territory. In a follow-up study of how war coalition partners chose future allies and enemies, again the temporal dimension was dominant, but contiguity was now considered as a major factor in dyadic behavior. A concern with conflict led naturally to questions about how conflicts grew and the diffusion of conflict; and this led—naturally—to an investigation of spatial factors and geopolitics broadly defined. These questions became a career-long interest, evidenced by the study of diffusion of international phenomena. In the past two decades, my geopolitical research was some of the first by international relations scholars to use GIS (geographical information systems). I used GIS in order to reconceptualize borders and apply data generated from that reconceptualization to questions of international conflict and cooperation.[2]

In distinction from a number of scholars of geopolitics (usually "realists" studying national security policy in some form) who see the geopolitical context at least as enduring—if not immutable or deterministic—I have been concerned with the *dynamism* of that context. Foucault once commented that scholars saw space as "the dead, fixed . . . immobile" (Agnew and Duncan 1989, 1). I have, however, argued that space or the spatial dimension is dynamic and changing. The realist Colin Gray (1977, 1) once asserted that "Geography is the most fundamental factor in the foreign policy of states because it is the most permanent." I argue that Gray's assertion tells only part of the story. Geography is important not just because of its relative stability, but also because of its role in shaping the dynamics of opportunities and risks. Geography affects the changing perceptions of the possibilities and probabilities provided by the environment. Although geography—in terms of topography or the absolute distance between two points, for example—is relatively stable, technological change or political change (such as that brought about by the creation or dissolution of alliances) alters the meaning and impact of geography on interaction opportunity and the structure of incentives and risks.

Crossing Boundaries

In my view, scholars—not only in international relations but across the subfields of political science—have pursued research more fruitfully when their theory and research designs "cross boundaries" of various kinds (see Starr 2006). Boundaries can indicate the limits of some set of phenomena; such simplification and specification can be valuable in the development of theory, concepts, and research design. However, boundaries too often loom as *barriers,* which can hinder how we think and theorize about phenomena and how we study the world about us. As analysts, we must be conscious of artificial boundaries or barriers that constrain our thinking and be just as conscious of finding ways to promote fertile theory and effective research design. In this sense, we should think of crossing boundaries as a synthesizing device that helps us in organizing theory and research.

The multiple, complex causal paths noted above have been generated by the realization that many, if not most, important questions in international relations have blurred the distinction between international relations and comparative politics. Both the external and internal contexts of states and other actors must be taken into account. Analysts have come to recognize and deal with the two-level nature of international phenomena and the network of internal-external linkages. To do so successfully we must cross boundaries. Included in this enterprise is the need to cross levels of analysis, to cross sub-disciplines, and, indeed, to cross disciplinary boundaries. Both external and internal contexts demand that we take advantage of other social science disciplines. In this volume, we will focus on the spatial context and the geographic factors that are important for understanding the choices of decision makers and the consequences of those choices—decision makers who sit within the internal environments of their states or other organizations, as well as within the international or global environment.

The Ecological Triad, Opportunity and Willingness, and Interaction Opportunity

A boundary-crossing approach is inherent in the opportunity and willingness framework. This framework, in turn, owes much to the ideas of the Sprouts. It would not be unfair to characterize a major thrust of the work of Harold and Margaret Sprout as an attempt to counter previous deterministic views and uses of geography. Although not the only perspective on geopolitics nor the only scholars to present that perspective, the Sprouts' version of possibilism has held a central place in the study of international relations.[3] Indeed, a group of "new geographers" concerned with the impact of geographic context has formed around the basic framework of Sproutian possibilism.

The Sproutian "ecological triad" is the mechanism by which we join politics and geography. This triad is composed of an entity, its environment, and the entity-environment relationship. The advantages of this framework derive from its applicability to any number of levels of analysis, and, thus, it crosses analysis boundaries. That is, whether the focus is on a single decision maker, a small group of decision makers, a foreign policy organization, a government as a whole, or the state as an international actor, the concept of the ecological triad argues that we need to look at the ongoing policy/choice processes within that entity, its context or environment, and then the interaction between the entity and the environment (see Friedman and Starr 1997). Determinism is only one form of the entity–environment relationship that could be hypothesized. However, it is a form in which the full causal force flows from the geographical environment to the human or institutional environed entities. In response to this model of the entity–environment relationship, the Sprouts argued the existence of alternatives where decision makers would be capable of making choices. One alternative was their construct of *environmental possibilism,* the central tenet of which

> is that the initiative lies with man, not with the milieu which encompasses him. Possibilism rejects the idea of controls, or influences, pressing man along a road set by Nature or any other environing conditions. The milieu, in the possibilist doctrine, does not compel or direct man to do anything. The milieu is simply there.... In the possibilist doctrine, the milieu is conceived as a set of opportunities and limitations. (Sprout and Sprout 1965, 83)

In this view, the environment is seen as a number of factors that limit human opportunities and that constrain the types of action that can be taken as well as the consequences of that action. Although the limits set by the environment may be wide or narrow, it is assumed that the limitations are discoverable. Once these limitations are known to some degree, another form of entity-environment relationship comes into play: *environmental probabilism.* As the humans in the decision units of any entity view their environment, the characteristics of that environment provide cues as to the probability of certain outcomes. The environment presents the entity not only with what is possible, but with what choices would be more or less likely under those particular circumstances.

If possibilism rests on the most basic notions of *choice,* elaborated by probabilism, in that some choices will be made more or less likely, then there is one more component that is essential to the Sproutian alternative to determinism: *cognitive behaviorism.* This is "the simple and familiar principle that a person reacts to his milieu as he apperceives it—that is as he perceives and interprets it in light of past experience" (Sprout and Sprout 1969, 45). This "psychological milieu" is about how humans see the environment and their images of the environmental context. Thus, the entity-environment relationship depends on the perceptions of the *entity*—a conception of the entity-environment relationship as far removed from determinism as possible (and quite congenial with more recent "constructivist" approaches). The "real" world has an impact only after choices are made and an implementation attempt is sent out into that real world. Note, however, that even the "feedback" from the real world somehow must be perceived in order to be learned and to affect future choices.

It should now be clear how the set of entity-environment relationships proposed by the Sprouts provided the basis of the opportunity and willingness framework. I have argued that *both* opportunity (possibilism) and willingness (probabilism and cognitive behaviorism) are *necessary* for understanding behavior: the environment must be permissive, and the acting unit must choose. As a pre-theory, the opportunity-willingness framework forces an analyst to take all three components of the ecological triad into account. The spatial and geographical components of the environment of any international actor are thus essential to understanding choice in foreign policy and international relations. Geopolitical factors compose an absolutely essential dimension of the environment that surrounds the whole range of entities that make

choices and act in world politics. The geopolitical environment includes the effects of space, topography, position, and
climate (Østerud 1988). Harold Sprout (1963) asserted that
geopolitical hypotheses deal with the configuration and layout of lands and seas, climate, and the distribution of natural
resources, as well as those dealing with the distribution of
people, social institutions, or behavioral patterns. Thus, all
international actors, or entities, may be located spatially—in
some geopolitical arrangement of typography and/or some
distribution of people, behavior, and resources.

Geopolitical factors in the environment thus provide
a *structure of opportunities and constraints.* The geopolitical
structure, including the geographic structure, is "always
both enabling and constraining," as Giddens (1984, 169) has
observed about structure in general. As developed in Starr
(1978) and Most and Starr (1989), opportunity consists both
of the possibilities that exist in the international system at any
point in history (e.g., technology, ideology, religion, social
inventions, such as new forms of government) *and* how those
possibilities are distributed in the system. Thus, there are two
dimensions to my version of possibilism. First, the phenomenon must already exist somewhere in the world system. The
phenomenon—be it nuclear weapons, telecommunications
satellites, Protestantism, Marxism, railroads, or financial
markets—must have been "invented" so that it is available as
a possibility to at least some actors in the system. The second
dimension centers on this possibility's distribution in the system. For example, nuclear weapons do exist; however, most
states cannot "take advantage" of them, because they have
neither the wealth nor the expertise to produce their own.
Though a possibility may exist, limits on resources affect the
ability to make use of it.

This second dimension is analogous to Harold Sprout's concern for the distribution of resources, people, or behavior, and also derives from the Sprouts' discussion of "capability analysis" (e.g., 1969, 53). The possibilities or opportunities that exist and their distribution help us understand both how costly or risky certain options appear to decision makers and how they might calculate the expected utility of those actions. That is, the geographic/geopolitical structure of opportunities and constraints (possibilism) are translated through environmental probabilism into the incentive structures of human beings who have to make choices. The geopolitical environment, then, has an impact on both opportunity and willingness, as people perceive the environmental opportunities and constraints, plug them into a structure of incentives that make choices more or less likely, and, through some form of utility calculations, have them affect the willingness to behave.

As noted, an important component of cognitive behaviorism is the set of geographic/geopolitical images that decision makers hold and how those affect their other images and calculations of choice. Decision makers' "mental maps" derive from geographic maps to form images of global and regional environments and the risks, threats, and opportunities in those environments (see Nijman 1991). Again, this follows on earlier work of Sprout and Sprout (1971, 248), who note that "maps are geographic models," and, as such, are simplifications that affect our images of the geographic/geopolitical environment (see Monmonier 1991; Akerman 2009).

The Sproutian alternatives to determinism, as combined in opportunity and willingness, also helped lead me to the interaction opportunity model of analysis of international behavior. One important question for geopolitical analysts is the selection of the appropriate contexts of interaction for study. In my studies of war diffusion, for example, starting at the level of the global environment for understanding the cues or prototypes of contagious behavior proved to be inadequate. These studies then moved to the neighbor level to find sets of states that were *important* (or relevant) to one another. Thus, the issue of salience is argued to be central to identifying a proper or useful "context" for interaction. For the study of war diffusion, neighbor effects (in the form of "warring border nations") were studied, as proximity to violent conflict was considered a major component of salience. In the study of the diffusion of democracy (Starr 1991), however, global and regional contexts, through demonstration effects similar to those found in the diffusion of innovations, were found to be more salient. Neighbor effects were clearly less important than in the diffusion of war.

A key issue in the interaction opportunity model, then, was *salience*: What makes one state important to another? For most issues, *proximity* of some sort is essential. One way in which proximity can be operationalized is in terms of geographic space, thus the focus on borders. Geographic proximity also provides an important element that affects behavior: ease of interaction. Based on the "First Law of Geography," or what G. K. Zipf (1949) called the law of least effort, ease of interaction means that entities physically closer to each other interact more than those farther away, because it is simply easier to do so. In international relations, the most important version of the distance-decay principle presented in the First Law of Geography was formulated by Kenneth Boulding (1962, 245), who looked at the "viability" of states in terms of a "loss-of-strength gradient" or "the degree to which [a state's] military and political power diminishes as we move a unit distance away from its home base."

Salience and ease of interaction together form the basis of the interaction opportunity model. The willingness of the decision makers of states to choose policy options—such as participation in a new war—will be based on perceptions of an environment changed by the behavior of "salient others," particularly others who are close by (and a greater threat to national security or viability). This approach thus identifies an impact on willingness through salience and perception of threat/importance, and on opportunity through possibilities for interaction and ease of interaction. Most and Starr's (1980) diffusion studies postulate that such interaction opportunities are a necessary condition for the diffusion of war and that they can also be used to indicate the direction of diffusion.[4]

In addition to indicating how geopolitical factors or environments at different levels of context can affect interaction, processes such as diffusion, or the occurrence of various types of events based on the interdependent choices of states, the interaction opportunity approach directs our attention to those phenomena or mechanisms that can *change* salience or the ease of interaction. For example, technology has been studied for the ways in which it has been used to overcome the spatial and temporal constraints of topography. Technology, or anything else in the environment that affects ease of interaction (and thus also salience), is able to change the *meaning* of the geographical/geopolitical context of environment. New technology permits humans to overcome physical barriers to the movement of ideas or things (especially military things) or to overcome the spatial distribution of resources through the creation of synthetic alternatives.

Later I will argue that alliances have a similar ability to change the impact and meaning of time and space, by "leap-frogging" physical barriers, such as mountains, oceans, or simply distance. These ideas are important in that they support the view that the geopolitical environment is *dynamic* in nature. The meaning of the geopolitical context can be changed rapidly through such mechanisms as technological innovation, the formation or dissolution of alliances, or the integration or disintegration of states. Far from a determinist view of the immutability of the earth's physical environment, the constraints of the environmental context (which would "determine" human choice and behavior) are being overcome by human technological invention or political innovation—thus changing what the physical environment means to decision makers in terms of the opportunities it presents and the probabilities of behavioral choices.

Conclusion

We have introduced a framework for understanding the relationships between international relations and geography. The following chapters will expand more fully on the components of this framework. In the next chapter, we will return to basics by looking at the nature and meaning of "space," spatiality, and distance, particularly as contrasted to time. We also introduce the important notion of "place."

CHAPTER 2
SPACES AND PLACES
THE POWER OF PLACE AND SPATIAL ANALYSIS

What Is There about Space?

Geographers would immediately notice that the title of this chapter combines the titles from the works of John A. Agnew (Agnew and Duncan 1989)—*The Power of Place*—and Luc Anselin (1999)—"The Future of Spatial Analysis in the Social Sciences." They would also recognize that these two scholars employ *very* different approaches to the study of geography, in terms of both methodology and epistemology. Despite those differences, however, when it comes to contrasting the importance of space and time to geographers in particular and to social scientists in general, both Agnew and Anselin appear to be in agreement.

It is Agnew and Duncan (1989, 1), on their first page, who cite Foucault as part of their argument that scholars need to take *place* seriously. In the words of Foucault,

> Space was treated as the dead, fixed, the undialectical, the immobile. Time, on the other hand, was richness, fecundity, life, dialectic.... The use of spatial terms seems to

have the air of anti-history. If one started to talk in terms of space that meant one was hostile to time. It meant, as the fools say, that one "denied history."

Similarly Anselin has stressed the contextual importance of space and that there has been a recent rekindling of attention to space across the social sciences:

> [A] relatively recent phenomenon is the renewed attention in the mainstream social sciences to geography in general, and location and spatial interaction in particular.... The distinct contribution of spatial analysis in this overall framework is that it provides the means to explicitly recognize, assess and incorporate the importance of location and interaction within the methodological toolbox of the social scientist. (1999, 67)

The same issues are raised by Goodchild et al. (2000, 140), who note,

> The analysis of space and place has become an increasingly pivotal component of social science research in the past two decades.... The centrality of space and place has always been taken for granted in geography and regional science. In contrast, in the mainstream of the social sciences, attention to the spatial (and space-time) dimension of phenomena is much less apparent, although a revival of sorts is occurring.

These scholars reflect a number of threads in geography that point out, and lament, the neglect of space and place in the social sciences. Looking at the study of international relations in general, as well as my main area of interest—the study of conflict and conflict processes—it is clear that despite some exceptions (the study of contiguity, for example), until very recently most of the research in these areas has stressed the temporal dimension or temporal context. This is easily seen in the design of research where temporal patterns are central, the use of time series data and designs is standard, and the use of time to delineate the units of analysis is also standard.[1] There is no denying the significance of time and the temporal context in social science. It is just as important, if we wish to be complete in contextualizing both our theory and the phenomena under investigation, to pay far more explicit and extensive attention to the spatial elements, or the spatial contexts, of social phenomena. In this chapter, we will discuss the importance of space, the relationship between space and time, how space and spatiality can be studied, and the continuing challenges of combining the study of space and time in our analyses of social phenomena.

"Space," as with all important concepts, is multidimensional. As introduced in the last chapter, and made explicit in the Sprouts' idea of "cognitive behaviorism," space is also a concept that takes on meaning only as it is perceived by individuals or groups of individuals. Thus, we must now introduce the idea of "place." Agnew and Duncan (1989, 2) provide three approaches to the idea of place. They note that geographers usually look at these separately, but that all three meanings are "complementary dimensions" of place. By looking at these three approaches, we can begin to highlight the meaning of space or spatiality:

> Approaches to defining a geographical concept of place have tended to stress one or another of three elements rather than their complementarity. Firstly, economics and economic geographers have emphasized *location,* or *space* sui generis, the spatial distribution of social and economic

activities resulting from between-place factor cost and market price differentials. Secondly, microsociologists and humanistic geographers have concerned themselves with *locale,* the settings for everyday routine social interaction provided in a place.[2] Thirdly, anthropologists and cultural geographers have shown interest in the *sense of place* or identification with a place engendered by living in it.

It should be noted that the first two approaches to place are clearly related to "opportunity." The third approach is related to "willingness," as part of identity and self-identification, of how people locate themselves in the universe, as well as how they value things.[3] The first approach—*location* or *space*—is the one with which I think students of international relations are most familiar, emphasizing the location of things in relationship to other things and how things are *distributed.* This idea of spatial contingency is picked up in Kirby and Ward's (1987, 3) definition of "spatiality" as "a contingent factor within the operation of any social formation," in which society's "components are themselves dependent upon their spatial setting."[4]

This view of place-as-location matches the two basic ways to think about location, as presented by Abler et al. in their classic text, *Spatial Organization* (1971, 59): "absolute location" and "relative location." According to Abler et al., "*Absolute* location is position in relation to a conventional grid system designed solely for locative purposes." In this view, location is provided by such things as latitude and longitude or a street address. The concept becomes much richer, but also much trickier, in the second way to think about location: "*Relative* location is position with respect to other locations." This can be expressed in terms of a variety of factors, such as distance or travel times from other locations, or the cost of such travel. Similarly, I have discussed how technology changes "relative location"—places that were once weeks apart in time are now only hours apart—and other mechanisms, such as alliances, can do likewise. As Abler et al. (1971, 82) note, "Any activity we undertake which makes it easier or more difficult for people, ideas, or objects to move through space *has significant effects* on spatial processes and the structures they produce" (emphasis added).

Abler et al. (1971, 72) note that prior to 1950, geographers generally dealt with space (and distance) in the "absolute" mode. Since then, however, in most research "relative location and relative distance has been used to define new kinds of stretchable, shrinkable spaces." Contrasting the two views, they note, "There are a large number of ways of describing distance and location in a relative context, but in the absolute context we are restricted to customary and unchanging units such as miles, kilometers, or degrees of latitude or longitude to measure distance" (1971, 59). In a view similar to the one I have expressed in my work, they note (in a way that would be at least congenial to Foucault) that, "human decisions constantly alter and restructure relative spaces. It has taken geographers a long time to challenge the pervasive tyranny of absolute space" (1971, 82).

Not only do human decisions "alter" relative spaces, various types of relative space explicitly take time into account, so that relative space and relative distance, and the *meaning* of relative space or distance, are heavily dependent on perceptions. Abler et al. note (1971, 75), "The spaces in which people live are much more psychological than absolute. If we are concerned, as we often are, with explaining spatial interaction, what is important is not how far two interacting places are from each other in absolute space, but rather how far the people at the two places *think* they are apart." This view captures the Sprouts' cognitive behaviorism, along with other "constructivist" models that have been developing for the last six decades, such as Snyder et al.'s (1954) "definition of the situation." In my own work, this involves how perception of space or distance affects willingness.

Although in recent decades the overwhelming focus has been on relative location and distance, geographers have not abandoned the traditional questions of geography: "Where?" and "*What* is where?" These questions—especially the latter—become more complex and interesting when dealing with relative distance. For example, in absolute space, using unchanging measures such as miles or kilometers—conceived of as Euclidian space—the shortest distance between two points is a straight line. Geographers, looking at relative space, have provided other ways to think about distances between two points, for example, a road that winds its way around a mountain. Similarly, cities where streets and avenues form grids that channel or constrain movement between the corners generated by the grid can be viewed as "Manhattan space." Abler et al. (1971, 73) note that Manhattan space is "a variant of Euclidian space, in which the shortest distance between two points is a path consisting of line segments which meet at right angles." Thus, a straight line as the shortest distance between two points, or "as the crow flies" distance, loses its meaning in a setting where a straight line is impossible. Manhattan space is a useful example of how any number of constraints can and do change the meaning of relative location or relative distance.

Types of Relative Space/Location

Earlier we introduced *place* as dependent on perception, identity, and values. We can now elaborate on that, using additional

Figure 2.1 Relative Locations in Relative Spaces

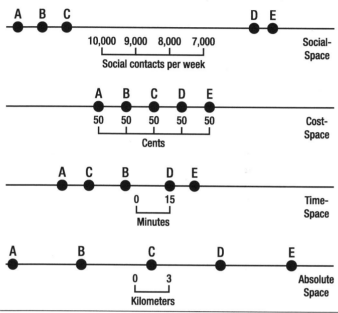

Source: Abler et al., 1971. Reprinted with permission.

ways to look at relative location or relative distance. Figure 2.1 is taken from Abler et al. (1971, 75). In it they provide four additional different ways in which space can be presented and thus contrast relative locations in relative spaces to the "reality" of absolute space. Figure 2.1 indicates how five separate points can *change* in their distances/location to each other based on absolute space, time-space, cost-space, and social-space. Using absolute space, each location—from *A* to *E*—is located six kilometers from its next neighbor. Location *A* is situated in absolute space six kilometers from location *B*, which is located six kilometers from location *C*, and so on, based on "a conventional grid system designed solely for locative purposes."

The other three types of space are relative spaces. "Time-space" is based on the amount of time it takes to go from one location to another (or move some object from one location to another). Whereas deterministic geopolitics is based on absolute location/distance, most of the questions we study in international relations regarding security, conflict, international political economy, or cooperation are based on time-space (and, as we shall see, cost-space). This is where technology has an important impact on how the meaning of space can change. In Figure 2.1, note that location C is now substantially closer to location A than location B. Such locations may flip for a number of reasons; for example, A may be closer to C in time-space because they are linked by an expressway, which shortens the time to drive between them, in contrast to the other locations, which are connected by winding, two-lane roads (or no roads at all!). Time-space is reflected in international relations' discussions of a "shrinking world." For example, we can track the pace of civilian intercontinental travel since the early nineteenth century. Around 1820, the earliest steamships traveled about 5 miles per hour. However, the transoceanic liner, RMS *Lusitania* (which figured so prominently in the US entry into World War I), which was launched in 1907, could travel approximately 30 miles per hour. The DC-3 airliner, introduced in 1936, had a maximum speed of approximately 230 miles per hour. But, only forty years later, following continually faster jet airliners, the Concorde supersonic airliner began flying commercially in 1976 with a speed just over Mach 2, or around 1,350 miles per hour! If we graphed these speeds, we would see a sharply accelerating exponential curve. Although the absolute location and distance between New York and London, for example, remained the same, the time–distance between them fell from about two months for the early transatlantic steamships to about three and a half hours for the Concorde. In the national security arena, we can find a parallel reduction of time-space with the development of intercontinental bombers and the subsequent development of intercontinental ballistic missiles (ICBMs). In any of these types of examples it is the *meaning* of distance that has changed in regard to human perception and choice.

Similarly, the *cost* of moving across distance has changed as well. Whereas time-space captures much of what Boulding (1962) meant by the "loss-of-strength gradient," "cost-space" captures the rest. Simply, cost-space deals with the costs of moving objects from one location to another. Cost-space is critical to what Agnew and Duncan (1989) meant when they stressed economics in discussing "location," dealing with "economic activities resulting from between-place factor cost." In Figure 2.1 cost-space is represented by the bus fare between locations. In the figure each location is equidistant from its neighbors—the bus ride costs $0.50 from location *A* to location *B,* and $0.50 from location *B* to location *C,* and so on. However, we also know that some public transportation systems are based on fare-stages, where the cost per absolute distance does not stay the same, so that fares are *not* proportionate to absolute distance; for example, the British bus system. Taxicab fares are based on cost-space, which includes the time it takes to get from location *A* to location *B* as well as the distance traveled—and sometimes within broad fare areas, so that, again, price is not based on the absolute distance traveled.

Just as changes in technology reduce the time it takes to move from one point to another, they also affect the costs of moving people and things. Not only must railroads be invented to become part of the menu of opportunities, but they must be available to any specific area if they are to reduce time and cost. Consider the cost of renting an apartment, or buying a house, near a commuter train station compared with one that is a thirty-minute drive away. Although closer in terms of time-space if moved by plane, some types of goods are closer (that is "cheaper") in cost-space if they move by rail, truck, or ship, owing to size or the amount that must be shipped to be economically worthwhile. Although Boulding's loss-of-strength gradient focuses on the time required to move military capabilities, cost-distance also highlights the economic and human costs of moving military capabilities. The cost of moving large numbers of troops has historically been high in terms of money and lives (with armies often losing more lives to disease, accidents, and hunger in long marches or sieges than in actual combat). The "projection of force," especially by major powers, using blue water navies, aircraft carriers, or long-distance bombers has often been much less costly than the movement of massive numbers of troops. The use of US air power in the first Gulf War is a most useful example. Again, a nuclear-armed ICBM also illustrates how technology can alter cost-space.

To indicate the variety of other possible relative dimensions, Abler et al. also include "social-space" in Figure 2.1, measured in terms of interactions, here the number of social contacts per week. Although locations might be close in terms of absolute space/distance, people may not interact proportionately with those who are closest. Social-space might reflect the different ethnic makeup of groups at specific locations or major class differences (which could be reflected in local prices and/or types of stores in the different areas). At this more micro level of analysis, we see this view of social-distance in the study of protracted social conflicts. As developed in the work of Edward Azar, protracted social conflict was a special form of social conflict that was long term and ongoing and permeated all aspects of the two societies involved. It was seen as highly intractable and apparently unresolvable to normal conflict resolution mechanisms because of the extensive linkages between development and violence that permeated the two actors. Classic cases of protracted conflict, the Israeli–Palestinian conflict and the conflict in Northern Ireland, also indicate that a key feature was conflict between the government of a state and at least one non-state actor on that state's territory. Gil Friedman (2002, 11) has noted that the typical protracted conflict situation finds the "geodemographic integration of rival nations," that is, the intermingling of peoples from different ethnic-national groups on the same territory. Thus, this constant opportunity for conflict is also embedded within a context of constant willingness. At the same time, individuals and groups that literally share the same territory have very low levels of interaction: although absolute distance is low, social-distance is quite high.

Social-space distances can also be found when looking at the international system in terms of a "feudal," or hierarchical, model. Studies of former colonial areas in the 1960s and 1970s revealed that they continued patterns of interaction that found former colonies interacting most with the former imperial power, next with other former colonies of that same imperial power, and far less with other states, even with their neighbors and near regions. In the 1960s and 1970s, for many Francophone African states, the quickest way to fly from one to another would be through Paris. The same relationships applied to former British colonies in Africa, where the quickest way to travel from one to another would be through London (e.g., see N. Gleditsch 1969). International relations scholars have also used social-space in looking for "distances" between states or groups based on any number of socio-political-economic factors. For example in Bruce Russett's (1967) study of regions, his analyses revealed homogeneous groupings of states that were "close"—that is were similar and clustered together—in terms of voting in the UN General Assembly, their networks of memberships in international organizations, trade interdependence, and sociocultural similarity. Looking across these analyses, we clearly find evidence that countries that were similar on one or more of these dimensions did interact more.[5]

As we can see, the various forms of relative space are ways of viewing space, place, and distance that help make the argument that geography and spatial approaches are dynamic and complex. One way this happens is because, "Individuals and groups of people live at intersections of numerous relative spaces" (Abler et al. 1971, 82). By noting these intersections, we can see the different ways space affects behavior as well as perceptions (and through perceptions, choice):

> Any activity we undertake which makes it easier or more difficult for people, ideas, or objects to move through space has significant effects on spatial processes and the structures they produce.... The number of dimensions we use and the way we measure distance along them determine the nature of any space we construct. By choosing different distance measures, we can change space. (Abler et al. 1971, 82, 73)

As we will see in Chapter 6, this task of developing "different distance measures" in order to *reconceptualize* space is exactly the aim of my work using GIS to remeasure and reoperationalize opportunity and willingness in regard to contiguous borders. In an absolute distance sense, contiguity indicates that two states touch. This is an on/off measure of contiguity that is relatively static unless the border is altered by war or diplomacy (e.g., integration, decolonization). By using GIS to develop indexes of ease of interaction (opportunity) and salience (willingness) that characterize any single border or any area along each border, variance has been added—variance that changes the nature and meaning of the border. The elements from the ARC/INFO GIS used to develop these indexes (discussed in Chapter 6) also demonstrate how human activity and creation can change borders and the meanings of borders beyond on/off touching—and might do so relatively quickly.

Space and Time and Space/Time Complementarity

Time and space are two of the primary ways in which we contextualize social behavior and interactions. Abler et al. (1971, 10) succinctly indicate the importance of these two dimensions: "Time and space are obvious and immediate aspects of human existence.... Time and space are the fundamental contexts of all experience.... Experience must be located in time and space before we can begin to process it further.... Locating an event in the spatio-temporal continuum is our first step in ordering our experience of it." Although this is rather obvious, it is key to understanding that *analyses structured solely (or almost entirely) around time are only telling us half of the story.* Let us return again to the question: Why is it that social scientists have been primarily concerned with time and only more recently turned to consider space?

There are some powerful differences in the ways in which time and space have been perceived and understood. These differences have enormous effects on how we think about phenomena and how we design our research to study international relations. The quotation from Foucault starkly outlines some of these differences—space as dead, fixed, immobile, whereas time was seen as rich and dialectic. Abler et al. (1971) provide one way of contrasting time and space, and examine how humans have considered them. Their argument allows us to turn Foucault's observation on its head. That is, in addition to the perceptual and analytical reasons found in discussing relative space, there are deeper reasons to argue that it is space that is richer and more complex, and thus deserves far more attention. Time is simply "easier" to deal with. Abler et al. observe,

> Because we cannot control our movement through time and because it is divided into formal units like days, lunar periods, years, we are *more aware of time* than space. Our consciousness of existing in time produces three regions along the temporal dimension: the past, the present, and the future.... At each moment we occupy a point in time. At that point, experience is very intense and immediate. Intensity and immediacy diminish as experience moves further into the past or as events we probably will experience move into an increasingly distant future. (1971, 8; emphasis added)

I think this is a powerful statement of why we are more aware of time. However, the "Western" linear temporal ordering of the past, the present, and the future—measured by standard units of time such as days or years—echoes the character and advantages of absolute space[6] (an ease of measurement and simplicity of conception that disappears with relative space). In contrast to this view of time, Abler et al. point out how we occupy space:

Spatially, we also occupy a nodal (central) position, although we have *no widely used categorization of space analogous to the division of time* into past, present, and future. Individuals and groups have *spatial ranges of various sizes,* but these have not been formalized in any generally accepted way.... All of us have territories and ranges and crudely formed conceptions thereof.... Perhaps our insensitivity to space is related to the fact that *movement in space is voluntary* whereas movement in time is wholly involuntary.... (1971, 9; emphasis added)

To develop the previous argument further, even absolute space with its standard units has no equivalent to the universal human experience with past, present, and future. All humans must be located physically somewhere (as noted, "no matter where you go, there you are"), but there are no common reference points. *All location is somehow relative and non-formalized.* The notion of movement through space being voluntary whereas movement through time is involuntary is crucial (if stunningly simple). Being more universal, more linear, and invariant (in the sense of its being involuntary), the temporal context is easier to understand and work into our research designs. Just *because it is voluntary,* the spatial context *should* be more important to many aspects of our research designs. However, there is no doubt that for other parts of research design, it makes our tasks much more difficult. I think this follows directly from the previous discussion of relative space/location and the complexities that can be found in even the simplest representation, such as in Figure 2.1.

It is because individuals and groups have different-sized spatial ranges and because all location is relative in some way that *place* (as in locale and sense of place) is so important to understanding human behavior in general and international relations in particular. We can now understand how place is so fundamental to group culture and identity (and to the self-identification of individuals). The most obvious examples are found in protracted conflicts, where two groups identify in the most profound sense with the same territory—the same place—and thus each wants exclusive rights to that place.

But we can also see less obvious examples of perception, place, and identity. Earlier I alluded to how maps can be used. The majority of the readers of this book would be most familiar with the typical Mercator projection map that places the United States at the center. This map splits Russia in two and also distorts large objects, especially landmass size, as one moves from the equator to the poles. The now-famous map of how the world would look with Australia in the central position is based on a map of Earth rotated 180 degrees from the point of view of someone living in the Southern Hemisphere. The world in such a map—as most of us (Northern Hemisphereans) picture it—looks to be a very different "place." In this Mercator projection, the United States is scrunched into the lower left-hand corner on top of an even more scrunched down version of Canada! (Go to http://flourish.org/upsidedownmap/hobodyer-large.jpg for a color version of this map.)

We do not need maps to see the ways in which people orient themselves to the geographical/spatial world. We note directly above how place gets caught up in the convergence of history and culture. In his discussion of "The Singularity of China," former Secretary of State Henry Kissinger notes, "While other countries were named after ethnic groups or geographical landmarks, China called itself *zhongguo*—the 'Middle Kingdom' or the 'Central Country'" (2011, 3). Chinese history as well as the perception of China by its leaders and people figuratively placed China at the center of any map of the region or the world.[7]

However, just as opportunity and willingness are jointly necessary conditions, time and space are jointly necessary dimensions of context. Each affects the other, and they are inexorably intertwined. Both need to be taken into account. As Michael Ward has argued, "nation-states operate in a thick context of time and space" (1991, vii). In a more general fashion Abler et al. (1971, 9) elaborate: "Because time is unidimensional, space is a part of our temporal continuum and vice versa. We can experience only one place at a time and moving from place to place consumes time. We are all of us nodes in personal space and time fields of experience, and as we move through time and space, we carry our nodality with us." We can also capture the time-space relationship using Abler et al.'s notion of "time-space convergence" (1971, 82–83). "Time-space convergence," they note, is about changes in relative location or relative distance, as captured by shorthand such as "a shrinking world.... We can monitor this shrinkage by measuring the *rates* at which *places* on the surface of the earth *approach one another in time distance*" (emphasis added). They note, "A peculiarity of time-space convergence is that distant places converge on each other at a greater rate than close places" (83). This reflects the impact that transportation technology has on spanning large distances more quickly, and the much more marginal improvements in moving across a city than across a continent or an ocean.

One example they present is looking at the time distance between Edinburgh and London in 1776 and then in 1966. The change that they found was based on the comparison of stage coach (5,760 minutes) to airplane (180 minutes). This yields a time-space convergence of 29.4 minutes per year.

That is, for each year between 1776 and 1966, the two cities became *closer* by an average of almost half an hour.[8]

We see then, why relative location/distance is so strongly focused on time-space, why it is so much oriented to how location and space relate to time and vice-versa. And, this is why technology and the range of other human invention are so important—by changing the meaning of space/location. Time-space and cost-space are about how long it takes to move objects across some distance, from some location to another, and the costs of doing so. They are crucial in our study of security, of military affairs, and thus to realist models of international politics. They are crucial in our study of economic, social, and political transactions; to our study of trade, diplomacy, and integration, and thus to liberal, neoliberal, and pluralist models of international politics. Thus time-space is central to our studies of international relations.

The Importance of "Place"

We should now understand why many geographers are paying greater attention to what "spatial reality" is, what it means, and the multiple ways scholars approach the geographic world. These are questions of geo-spatial ontology that are similar to those scholars of international relations would recognize as being raised by constructivist approaches to social scientific investigation, for example.[9] Antony Galton gets to the heart of the matter quickly and simply:

> Everything I see on a map can be described as geographical information. It is obvious that such information comes in many different forms. Representing a town by

placing a small circle at a specific location on the map is quite different from showing the extent of woodland by coloring areas of the map green. How should the different kinds of geographical information be classified? Can we divide them into a small number of basic kinds, or are we faced with a plethora of uniquely different sorts of information that resists any attempt at systematization? If we settle for a few basic kinds, how are these kinds related, and how should we decide which kind to use in any particular case? (2001, 173)

What this quote tells us is that we must explicitly recognize the psychological aspects of place, distance, their meanings, and how those meanings can change. We need to extend political psychology to concerns that we might have previously called political geography, and vice versa. Thus, we must continue to stress that such meanings are *dynamic* and that geographic contexts are not immutable constant factors in our research. Such approaches can have a significant impact, for example, on studies of ethnic conflict and especially on the study of protracted social conflict. One challenge will be not only to look at absolute distance, as in the presence or absence of contiguity, but how territory is viewed by leaders, populations, and relevant subsets of these populations. The spatial distribution and locations of such subsets of people should be examined as well.

A Final Note: How to Study Spatiality?

We began this chapter with a reference to the work of Luc Anselin and will conclude it with his contributions as well. Anselin (1999, 68–69) has noted that, "the 'geographical perspective,' or *thinking spatially* also has an important role to play in the refinement of the way in which space is incorporated into social science itself." Anselin has provided important guidelines for our thinking about space, for the integration of spatiality into our analyses, and for the creation of methods to study space that need to be added to our analytic "toolbox." Pulling together spatial thinking as well as methodology, Anselin (1999, 70) presented scholars of international politics with three "broad challenges":

1. "the concept of *space* itself, how it is incorporated in statistical models (regression models in particular) as well as stored in digital form in a GIS. The standard approach is to treat space as a container for spatial objects or as a field by means of which spatial distributions are described."
2. "the need to provide a meaningful theoretical interpretation for the *role of 'space'* as it is incorporated in spatial statistical and spatial econometric models." Is it contiguity, or a "spatial multiplier effect"?
3. "[the] more technical challenge to spatial analysis is to develop data models and modeling techniques to handle spatial interaction as well as *space-time interaction*. Especially in the context of theoretical models of diffusion and contagion, a proper metric for the distance in space-time (or speed of diffusion) is required."

To address these analytical challenges, Anselin has presented three important ways in which spatial analysis contributes to the social scientist's toolbox. The first deals with "data integration," which involves "the conversion of data collected at one spatial scale (and time dimension) to other scales and dimensions. Specifically, this is needed when geo-locational information must be manipulated or when spatial data must be obtained for locations or areal units for which they are not originally recorded" (Anselin 1999, 68). This need has both generated the increased use of GIS across the social sciences and has been driven by the increased availability of spatial data produced by GIS (as can be seen in Chapters 6 through 8).

Political geography, then, also provides the possibility for a variety of new data sets for the study of international phenomena. Looking at space as well as various subdivisions of that space is one strategy by which to increase the number of observations in what have previously been small-N studies (for example, see Collier 1993). GIS has generated a large amount of new data about the world and how it is organized, such as the unified spatial data structure of PRIO-GRID (Tollefsen et al. 2012). Students of international relations need to identify such data and make use of them, as well as design new GIS-based studies to develop data sets that would have been unavailable without GIS technology.

In part based on the nature and power of GIS, the second important contribution involves "exploratory spatial data analysis (ESDA) and visualization in an inductive approach to discovering patterns, eliciting hypotheses and suggesting associations" (Anselin 1999, 68). The third important contribution involves the use of deductive approaches to analyze the spatial context: "When the empirical work is based on spatial (cross-sectional) data or when the models under consideration are 'spatial' in nature (spatial interaction), an application of the specialized methodology of spatial statistics and spatial econometrics is required" (1999, 68).[10] Spatial data analysis tools therefore permit exploration of data from a spatial perspective, looking for spatial patterns, correlations, outliers, and residuals and submitting apparent patterns to rigorous statistical tests. They also permit the confirmatory testing of nonspatial hypotheses, using spatial data. This brief discussion only provides the most cursory taste of the range and power of current methodologies to study the effects of, and role of, spatiality in our analyses. But it does highlight the challenges of how to study space and spatiality and the even more difficult challenge of combining spatial and temporal contexts/perspectives/modes of analysis.

Conclusion

Before moving on to discussions of the intersection between geography/geopolitics and international relations, it was necessary to provide a common set of ideas and concepts—a common foundation for understanding the nature of geopolitics. One central purpose of Chapter 2 was to do just this, introducing the basic ideas of space, place, location, and distance. It is important to understand how each of these ideas is different from the others, but also how they affect how each of the other ideas takes on *meaning,* as well as the synergy among them. We have also provided a basic outline of how these ideas might be studied and the tools that geography can provide to scholars of international relations. In so doing, we have also been able to demonstrate the dynamism of geography/geopolitics. This is a view that is quite distinct from earlier deterministic realist views of geopolitics, and one much more in tune with current theoretical perspectives of international relations.

Chapter 3
Territory, Proximity, and the Geography of International Conflict

Cumulation and International Conflict

Building on the last chapter, here I will present an overview of the ways in which space, spatiality, and proximity are theoretically important, for example, in the examination of international conflict behavior, to agent-structure models of opportunity, diffusion, the loss-of-strength gradient, and the effects of distance-space. The opportunity and willingness framework is used to organize both the literature and the discussion that builds on Paul Diehl's (1991) seminal overview of geography and conflict. I wish to review several broad approaches to the study of geopolitics and international conflict and ways to tie studies of the geography of conflict together as well as present some observations on productive methods for the study of spatial/geographic aspects of international conflict.

It is hoped that through such an exercise, the odds of generating cumulation—especially Dina Zinnes's (1976) idea of "integrative cumulation"—will be greatly improved. As noted in Most and Starr (1989, 7), for Zinnes,

> additive cumulation occurs when "one study adds some in-
> formation to the existing literatures on the subject," through
> such activities as the citation of previous findings, using
> previously collected data, secondary or reanalysis of existing
> data, the incorporation of new cases or new variables into
> the analysis, or expanding the application of models, indices
> or techniques to new cases or research questions.

Integrative cumulation goes further, reflecting instances
where earlier studies are, "'crucial' to the conceptual and
theoretical components of the subsequent study's research
design. Additive cumulation should not be slighted, however,
in that it is an indispensable part of the process that leads to
integrative cumulation.[1]

Territoriality, proximity, and spatiality have all played
central roles in the study of international conflict. The place
of territory in the analysis of conflict and the study of the
diffusion of conflict are two areas where there has been
considerable "additive cumulation." This is especially true
regarding the use of border data sets such as the extensive and
detailed data set compiled by the Correlates of War project (go
to www.correlatesofwar.org/). Additive cumulation is also
found in the widespread use of contiguity as an independent
or control variable in the study of conflict across different
units of analysis (monadic, dyadic, and regional analyses),
different time periods, and for different types of conflict (for
example, war only, or events lower on the escalatory ladder
as tapped by the Militarized Interstate Dispute, or MID,
data). The concept of "nice laws" (Most and Starr 1989)—or
domain-specific laws—suggests that we should be concerned
with under what conditions certain theories hold. In doing
so, activities like those just noted that indicate additive cumulation become important and useful in specifying theory.

Given the extensive set of factors in the area of political geography that has led to additive cumulation, it is important to note that examination of the place of territory in the analysis of conflict and the study of the diffusion of conflict have also demonstrated a growing "integrative cumulation." The argument for cumulation in these areas has been presented in a set of overview works on the role of territory and of diffusion studies (for example, see Most et al. 1989). Indeed, except for the research program on the democratic peace, few other areas in the study of conflict have developed such consistent, complementary, and reinforcing sets of empirical findings (see, for example, Hammarstrom and Heldt 2002). We find that contiguity has become a standard component of models since its inclusion as one of the handful of factors in Stuart Bremer's (1992) famous identification of "dangerous dyads." *How* territory, proximity, and spatiality have promoted integrative cumulation in the study of international conflict will be addressed in the remainder of this chapter.

Space, Territory, and International Conflict

Students of international relations have developed unusually coherent and useful overviews of theoretical and empirical work that relate the study of international politics/conflict to geography, territory and territoriality, distance, space, and spatiality. Although the overarching idea that holds all of these works together is that of the *spatiality* of phenomena, overviews of spatiality by scholars who are *not geographers* have appeared only relatively recently. Much of my own thinking about space and spatiality, borrowed from geographers, was presented in the previous chapter—especially in discussing the differences among such concepts as space, location, and distance and their interrelationships.

Returning to the issue of integrative cumulation and how theory develops, it can be argued that students of international relations have been concerned with distance for two broad theoretical and conceptual reasons. Conveniently, these two reasons can be summarized as *opportunity* and *willingness*. First, distance is important because states (or any other social units) that are close to each other, that is, are in proximity to one another, are better able to interact. Simply, they have the possibility or opportunity of interacting with one another—the "interaction opportunity" argument or approach discussed in Chapter 1. Again, as noted, the second reason why we should be concerned with distance is willingness: States (or any other social units) that are close to each other are also *perceived* as important or salient to each other. Greater perceptions of threat or gain, or of interdependence, are ways in which proximity can generate salience. Such views affect willingness through the expected utility calculations of policy makers. Willingness to interact and to manage subsequent conflicts in different ways, for example, will depend on the importance or salience of an issue or an opponent.

Thus, proximity makes states (or other social units) that are close to one another "relevant" to one another through some combination of both opportunity and willingness. High levels of opportunity and willingness—generated, for instance, by long, contiguous borders that go through areas with valuable resources and important strategic features, and on both sides of which live members of the same ethnic group—mean that two states are easily able to interact with each other and both perceive the other as important and relevant (whether as a possible opponent or cooperator through shared interests).

This presentation becomes more important when we look at the way many research designs to study international conflict are constructed. Students of international conflict have structured research designs to include only "relevant" dyads—pairs of states that are able to interact with one another, highly likely to interact with one another, or perceive important stakes involved in that interaction (e.g., Leeds and Davis 1999; Lemke and Reed 2001). They have developed studies based on states within politically relevant areas or neighborhoods, such as Zeev Maoz's "politically relevant international environment" or PRIE (1996). New work on "network" analyses of various kinds (for instance, Maoz 2010, 2012) or K. Gleditsch's (2002) "connectivity matrix" analysis extends the concept and utility of actors who are "relevant" to each other through spatial or behavioral proximity and the ways network approaches can be applied to international relations. As Mats Hammarstrom and Birger Heldt (2002, 358) explain, "the term 'network' refers to a set of units of some kind and the 'ties' (relations) of specific types that occur among them." Not only can such ties or relations be represented spatially, but they are often dependent on the actual spatial arrangement of the social units. For example, using "network position," Hammarstrom and Heldt (2002) support previous findings on the diffusion of conflict among contiguous states, but also argue that the network position approach allows them to identify *which* contiguous states are most likely to be the sites of diffusion.

Now let's add territory. There is an additional factor in the relationship between proximity and the *stakes* of interaction. If we are talking about states, we are talking about *territorial* units. States are proximate to one another in a spatial or geographic manner if their territorial areas are near each other. How close or far are these territorial areas from each other in terms of absolute distance? Are they contiguous? That is, do the territories of two states *touch* each other? Do they *border* each other? If they do not actually touch each other, are they separated by rivers? If they do not actually touch each other, how far apart are they across some other body of water? Thus, borders represent the highest level of proximity—the touching of territory or, by dictionary definition, the condition of contiguity (see Starr and Most 1976; and Chapter 4 this book).[2]

It should be clear that territory serves at least two distinct purposes in the study of international relations. First, by defining the territorial extent of political units, territory creates spatial arrangements among the units, indicating the physical/geographic distance between those units. As seen in the previous chapter, this "distance" is dynamic, in that the *time-distance* between the units changes with changing technologies of transportation and communication, with changes in the arrangements of the units through alliances, or with the merging of units through conquest or voluntary integration. The conquest of territory can create new borders (as in the expansion of Russia or the United States across their respective continents or the Napoleonic expansion across Europe). The breakup of states or empires can create new borders—as in the post-USSR or post-Yugoslavian situations or the redrawing of the world map after World War I, with the dissolution of the Ottoman, Russian, and Austro-Hungarian empires. But, borders were also altered with the reunification of Germany after the fall of the Berlin Wall and dissolution of the Warsaw Pact. Voluntary integration, as seen in the progressive growth of the European Union (both geographically and functionally) can also change the legal, economic, and political nature and meaning of borders.

Second, we have also discussed the importance of *place* and the way territory provides an important component of *group identity* and becomes endowed with extraordinary symbolic importance to people. Large numbers of geographers are concerned with the symbolic importance inherent in territory and the role such symbolism/identity plays in the daily lives of people as well as international politics. In addition to value based on symbol and identity, territory may also provide real resource value to peoples (arable land; potable water; minerals of value such as gold, uranium, or oil; access to seas or rivers; and other features of militarily strategic value). So, territory takes on value across many dimensions. *Territory is important to humans* across all levels of social aggregation. It both becomes a source of conflict and raises the stakes of any conflict.

These broad ways by which territory becomes related to conflict—again through opportunity (ease of interaction) and willingness (importance or salience)—have been addressed by a number of scholars in literature reviews or as part of specific research projects. Perhaps the most influential of these pieces was by Paul Diehl (1991), who presented geography as both a facilitating condition for conflict and as a source of conflict. This dichotomy has served as the basis for subsequent reviews and empirical research, with scholars building on his broad categorization of the two basic ways territory becomes part of the international conflict process (see also Vasquez 1993; Huth 1996; and Hensel 2000, 2012).

Opportunity, Willingness, and Ordering Spatial/Geographic Effects

We have already discussed how the opportunity and willingness framework can help represent the importance of distance as well as the effects of territory in international politics. We will now use opportunity and willingness to further explore how territory/geography is related to conflict. But in so doing, we will also be returning to the initial development of opportunity and willingness as a way to help synthesize and bring order to large (and sometimes unwieldy) literatures (see Starr 1978). As with the general study of conflict, the concepts of opportunity and willingness can be useful in organizing literatures and making sense of disparate studies and approaches as well as serve minimally as pre-theoretic devices for generating hypotheses, conceptualizing components of our theories or models, and searching for nonintuitive relationships (see Most and Starr 1989; Cioffi-Revilla and Starr 1995).

Opportunity and willingness is a form of agent-structure model, initially created to deal with the ways in which "entities" are related to their systemic environments. To go back to basics, interdependence is a quality of systems. Systems are composed of units of some kind and the interaction among them. In the simplest of terms, we must be concerned with each unit and how each unit adapts to its environment. This individual adaptation produces the patterns of interaction that characterize the system. The Sprouts' ecological triad described earlier informs any agent-structure approach and helps us think about units and their environments. Ultimately, we are concerned with the possibilities and constraints that face decision makers (opportunity) and with the choices that they make in light of these possibilities and constraints (willingness). The various levels of analysis involved in the study of international relations are thus linked by thinking of a decision maker as an entity who must behave within the very complex environment that surrounds him or her. Each level of analysis used in the exploration of international politics and foreign policy (for example, idiosyncratic/psychological, role/

organizational, governmental, societal, dyadic or relational, regional, systemic) describes one of the environments within which the decision maker must operate.

To summarize, opportunity requires three related conditions: (1) an environment that permits interaction between states, (2) states that possess adequate resources to be capable of certain kinds of actions, and (3) decision makers, or human agents of some kind, who are aware of both the range of interactions and the extent of capabilities available to them. Opportunity is the possibility of interaction because of objective conditions that may be perceived in varying (more and less accurate) ways by decision makers. Willingness is concerned with the motivations that lead people to avail themselves of opportunities. Willingness deals with the goals and motivations of decision makers and focuses on why decision makers choose one course over another. Willingness thus depends on choice and perception.

Finally, as argued earlier, it is important to understand that *both* opportunity and willingness are required for a given behavior to occur; they are jointly necessary conditions. Wishing for something to happen is not enough—the capabilities (of whatever kind) to act for its fulfillment must be available. Simply being able to do something doesn't mean it will happen unless you have the will to take action (see especially Cioffi-Revilla and Starr 1995).

Geography as a Facilitating Condition

Let us now return to the relationships between geography and conflict as well as territory and conflict. Recall that territory reflects the spatial location of states, including their proximity or distance from one another—with their contiguous borders representing the highest level of proximity. We have also indicated some of the reasons why proximity or distance and territory are important. We can return to these basic issues using Diehl's (1991) discussion assessing the work on geography and war. This work is important because of the manner in which Diehl categorizes the literature. He breaks the empirical studies of geography and war into two groups: (1) "geography as a facilitating condition" for conflict, and (2) "geography as a source of conflict."[3]

The work of Starr and Most (1976) specifically looked at the importance of proximity and how it was measured and represented by borders and territory. Their diffusion research project (Most and Starr 1980) moved to examine borders after concluding that the diffusion of certain phenomena was best studied by looking only at units that were "relevant" to one another, with relevance indicated by geographical proximity. Proximity, in turn, could be operationalized through "borders." Diehl in fact uses the work of Starr and colleagues to illustrate the category of "geography as a facilitating condition" for conflict. In this research, Most and Starr developed the idea of *interaction opportunity* as introduced earlier. In Most and Starr's terms, the closer units such as states are to one another, the greater their possibility for interaction.

The opportunity for interaction concept was elaborated by Siverson and Starr (1991). They conceptualized proximity, as measured by borders and contiguity, as a factor of "loose necessity." That is, proximity creates the possibility for conflict through increased possibilities for interaction (both positive and negative); thus, it raises the probability of interactions, both positive and negative. They stress the basic idea that the interaction opportunity model *only* holds that closer units will *interact more*. However, many (if not most) scholars have assumed that greater interaction leads to more conflict and, in turn, their studies have been designed to apply the interaction opportunity idea to conflict rather than coopera- tive behavior. Such an approach is clearly a misunderstand- ing of possibilism as well as opportunity. Zipf's "law of least effort" applies to interactions in general, positive as well as negative. Diehl (1991) understood this distinction, meaning that proximity of territory only increases the probability of conflictual interaction but does not ensure it will happen.

Likewise, Siverson and Starr (1991) found that borders (as well as alliances) only increase the probability that ongoing wars will diffuse from "warring border nations," not that they necessarily will do so. Similar results abound. For example, Maoz and Russett (1992, 260) have observed that, although contiguity is a strong factor in predicting dyadic conflict, "it does not account for the relative lack of conflict between democratic states." And, of course, none of the arguments for the interaction opportunity apply *only* to territorially proximate homelands. Starr and Most (1976) raise the issue that territorially proximate *possessions* of states will have the same effects. In addition, the interaction opportunity argu- ment (based on the loss-of-strength gradient) also recognizes that "great" or "major" powers are so named because they possess a greater ability to interact with states far from their homelands. These states can project military power globally so that their interaction opportunities have transcended first- order territorial contiguity.[4]

It is also clear from some of my later studies that high interaction opportunities may lead to more cooperative behavior as well as conflictual behavior. Starr and Thomas (2002, 2005) found that high levels of ease of interaction across borders—greater interaction opportunities—are also related to positive interdependence/integration effects. Starr and Thomas (2005) argue that simply categorizing two states as being contiguous may not adequately reflect expected underlying behavior. They present two different views on the relationship between contiguity and conflict: (1) interaction opportunity, which is hypothesized to make conflict more probable, and (2) Karl Deutsch's social communication model of integration that contends increased interactions, transactions, and interdependence make conflict less probable. Each view, however, represents a linear (positive or negative) relationship between ease of interaction and conflict. To deal with this problem, Starr and Thomas (2002, 2005) propose a curvilinear relationship with the *low occurrence of conflict* at both the lowest and highest levels of ease of interaction (opportunity) and salience (willingness). Conflict is most likely where the expected utility of conflict is greatest—that is, in the middle—where states have *both* the opportunity and willingness to engage in conflict.

These observations stress the importance that those studying territory and proximity correctly understand the arguments behind interaction opportunity/ease of interaction as a facilitating condition. As a form of opportunity, the facilitating condition argument starts with the idea that it must be *possible* to interact, to have conflict, and to have militarized conflict. Proximity both creates such possibilities and raises their probabilities (and also raises the probability of cooperative interactions under the *right circumstances*). But, proximity is only *one* of a number of other potentially *substitutable* ways by which these possibilities occur! Most and Starr (1989) have observed that opportunity or willingness can operationally occur or be made available in a number of alternative, nonunique, and substitutable ways. Substitutability, then, refers to the existence of a set of alternative modes of response or "alternative modes of redundancy" (Cioffi-Revilla and Starr 1995, 456–457) by which decision makers can deal with some situation. Again, proximity is just one of the substitutable modes to increase interaction opportunities. *Any factor that affects the meaning of distance,* especially time-distance, can become such a substitutable mechanism. Technology provides many such mechanisms. For example, possibilities for interaction with a power projection that is low in cost exist for states with long-range nuclear armed missiles or aircraft carrier–based bombers.

Geography as a Source of Conflict

The work on geography, territory, or the "territorial perspective"—where territory acts as the cause, the source, or the stakes involved in conflict—is quite extensive. Diehl (1999, x) reviews the value or importance of territory, or what he calls the tangible "intrinsic importance of territory," including such items as natural resources, control over populations, access to trade, and strategic value. More intangible or symbolic aspects of territory are also included, such as its historic value and its relationship to the group identity/ethnicity of the people living on it. David Newman (1999, 14) sees territory as a "demographic container" that holds people, providing territorial symbolism to their identity, such that territory becomes an "exclusive entity" for a people. This view creates a powerful we/they or us/them divide regarding territory and is vital to models based on the cohesion of social groups (for an overview of social-psychological theories, see Pruitt and

Kim 2004). For instance, Cameron Thies (2001) has linked territory as an issue to the factor of national identity, discussing how this connection helps to generate and maintain an enduring rivalry.

Given the variety of factors that give territory value, it is not surprising that territory serves as the origin of conflict. It does so through territorial claims (Hensel 2001), territorial changes (Kacowicz 1994), territorial disputes and their settlement (Huth 1996; Huth and Allee 2002; Sample 2002), and strategic concerns, among others. Paul Huth (1996) has used territorial disputes to demonstrate how domestic factors interact with such disputes and to modify realist geopolitical theories. An interesting twist on the strategic importance of territory is found in John Vanzo (1999), who is concerned with the configuration of borders, especially the notion of the "compactness" of states. Similarly, Elliott Green (2012) has investigated the size and shape of African states and concludes that they are not the "arbitrary" colonial artifacts many observers assume. Thomas Christin and Simon Hug (2012) have looked at the interaction of the structure of federalist states, the location of different identity groups, and internal conflict.

Many students of international relations have presented arguments for, and reviews of, empirical findings regarding territory/geography as a source of conflict (e.g., Holsti 1991; Vasquez 1993; Hensel 2000; and Huth 1996). One illustrative empirical study by Vasquez and Senese (2003) indicates that territorial claims increase the probability that a pair of states will engage in a militarized dispute (MID) and that such territorial MIDs, in turn, increase the probability of war. A review of the continuously updated set of contemporary armed conflicts by Peter Wallensteen and his colleagues for the Uppsala University UCDP/PRIO data set also reveals the extent to which territorial issues continue to underlie international conflict in the post–Cold War era. For example, 151 of the 248 "armed conflicts" identified between 1946 and 2011 (or 61 percent) involved territory as the "incompatibility" in the conflict (see the data sets listed at www.pcr.uu.se/research/ucdp/datasets/ucdp_prio_armed_conflict_dataset/). Clearly territory (or geography) as a source of conflict falls under both opportunity and willingness.

Territory that connects, sits between, or is disputed by two states provides something to fight over. This is not simply a facilitating condition. Territory exists as a possible issue for conflict; it is available as a source of conflict or contention. Because of territory's value, however—both tangible and intangible—territory is something that people care about and are willing to fight over and is directly connected to willingness. People, groups, and states come into conflict every day during the course of normal social transactions and interactions: Incompatibilities occur, representing incompatible claims of interests and preferences. Most such incompatibilities are managed simply through routine mechanisms or are ignored because they do not make claims to things that are highly valued. The research on territory and conflict indicates that territory is literally always of high value, salience, or importance to people and groups. Territory raises the stakes/value of conflict, thus raising the probability of escalation and lowering the probability of easy management. This is also demonstrated by looking at conflict management from the opposite perspective. Recent research (Gibler and Tir 2010) has shown that when countries *do settle* border disputes through treaties that establish agreed boundaries, such settlement leads not only to peace but to democracy (see also Owsiak 2012). The same effects accompany boundary river treaties (Tir and Stinnett 2011; Bernauer et al. 2012).

Because territory is of such value, it increases the expected utility of fighting for it, even if the probability of success appears to be low. Hensel (2000), for example, explicitly links territory to such expected utility considerations. This is a key reason why territory and contiguity are regularly used as independent, intervening, or control variables in models of international conflict. It is important to note that, just as with territory as a facilitating condition, the argument here is not that territory is the only, or even the most important, source of conflict across all situations or under all conditions (see, for example, Mitchell and Prins 1999, who demonstrate this observation when investigating the issues at stake in the study of militarized disputes). However, what the work of Diehl, Vasquez, Hensel, Huth, and others mentioned earlier has shown is that territory is often the central issue at stake and should be included in the group of "usual suspects."

Perhaps the study of protracted social conflicts best represents all of these points. In Gil Friedman's (2002) terms, as noted earlier, the typical protracted conflict situation finds the "geodemographic integration of rival nations," that is, the intermingling of peoples from different ethnic/national groups on the same territory. This constant opportunity for conflict is also embedded within a context of constant willingness. The conflicting claims over the ownership of the territory are claims representing the highest values for each group, because the ownership of the territory is passionately attached to or embedded in group identity. The constant, and high, level of both opportunity and willingness is a significant factor in the intractability of protracted social conflicts.

The relationship between the value of territory and international conflict can also be explained by prospect theory (or, more specifically, the prospect theory variation of expected utility models; see, for example, Levy 2000). Prospect theory introduces the idea of "endowment effects," where, "because of loss aversion, people tend to value what they have more than comparable things that they do not have" (Levy 2000, 195). The new acquisition of territory (because it is so highly valued) produces almost immediate endowment effects. Because of these endowment effects, when a country takes territory, we find that *both* sides now frame the situation as one of losses. That is, the state that has lost territory frames the situation as one of loss, becoming risk acceptant in terms of the escalation or pursuit of the conflict. In effect, the state that has newly acquired territory now claims the territory and also quickly frames any return of the territory in the realm of losses. Thus, both sides frame the situation as involving losses. In turn, both sides become risk acceptant with regard to the escalation or militarization of the conflict. Thus, there is increased willingness and an increased probability of escalation to militarized conflict!

As has been noted, behavior cannot occur without both opportunity and willingness. Opportunity can be created by a number of "second-order substitutable mechanisms" (see Cioffi-Revilla and Starr 1995). Spatial proximity (for example, through contiguity) is one such mechanism. Thus, geography or territoriality as a facilitating mechanism is not a contending model with geography/territory as a source of conflict. As the two models represent opportunity and willingness, both must be present. The facilitating condition makes conflict possible, increases its probability, but does not guarantee that it will occur.

Conclusion

As I have previously noted,

> Cumulation and "progress" in the study of global phe-
> nomena will depend on the quality and rigor of our
> theories and our methods. Synthesis will follow broad
> agent–structure approaches that cut across more standard
> levels of analysis and disciplinary boundaries. The chal-
> lenges facing researchers arise from finding the appropriate
> methods by which to study the agent–structure problem.
> (Starr 2002b, 370)

I have also discussed a set of challenges facing IR scholars, including questions of how to cut into the continuous feedback
loops between agent and structure (between endogenous and
exogenous factors). For research on international conflict to
meet the stringent criteria of integrative cumulation, we will
also need to meet the challenge of how to include the study
of space and spatiality and the even more difficult challenge
of combining spatial and temporal contexts/perspectives/
modes of analysis.

CHAPTER 4
INTERNATIONAL BORDERS IN AN AGE OF GLOBALIZATION

"Place" in the Westphalian System

As we have discussed space and place, we have seen the importance of location and place. Location is about how things are arranged and sit in relation to other things, whereas place captures the meaning people give to specific locations. However, we have looked at place mostly from the point of view of substate groups and the individuals that make them up. States are territorial entities, and borders allow people to see what territory belongs to what state. What does place mean in regard to states in the current Westphalian system of territorial states? What do territory and borders mean regarding location and place in a globalized world where people, things, and information seemingly move about without constraint? Are borders still important? How?

Borders do matter. Even in today's "turbulent," post–Cold War world of growing democracy, interdependence, and globalization, borders still serve a wide variety of functions across the areas of security, economics, politics, and social interactions. Even with a broad set of contemporary challenges to sovereignty, borders delineate areas of legal competence. Borders encompass the territoriality necessary to the concept of the state. They provide a key element in the structure of the global system—mapping the number and arrangement of the territorial units upon which all humans live. Thus, borders are central to a spatial approach to international politics, by setting out the location and arrangement of states and their distances from one another. Borders both facilitate and constrain human interaction. They continue to be intimately related to the security of states and the analysis of interstate conflict, but affect interstate cooperation as well.

Realist/Legal Notions of Borders

Broadly, the concept of "border" has been an important one throughout world history, and especially so for the past five hundred years and since the development of the state-centric, sovereignty-based Westphalian state system. Two significant ways to view borders between sovereign nation-states derive from realist approaches to international relations. The first way involves borders as *legal* phenomena—the legal boundaries that were provided to the nation-states that emerged subsequent to the Thirty Years War. These states were seen to have a *territoriality* dimension that had been lacking in the system of feudal organization that it replaced. Common usage sets out the Treaty of Westphalia in 1648 as the beginning of the modern state system. Prior to Westphalia (and the Protestant Reformation), the system that existed in western Europe was composed of two ideal hierarchies, and politics revolved around *multiple loyalties*. One hierarchy was religious—the Catholic Church, with the pope at the apex. The other hierarchy was secular, founded on the feudal ideas of fealty (or loyalty) that flowed upward, with the Holy Roman emperor at the apex. Any individual, peasant, knight, or lord owed fealty to the immediate level above and all levels above that. With the Treaty of Westphalia, states were created with a unique, again ideal, legal status of sovereignty that depended on borders.

The Treaty of Westphalia in 1648 gave the ultimate political authority to the "prince" of a given territorial unit, rather than the pope or the Holy Roman emperor. The legal condition of sovereignty gave the prince's government complete control over the territory and people on that territory, with no external authority having the legal right to order the state how to act. The state's boundaries determined the crucial *legal* boundaries between what was internal (or domestic) and external (or the realm of foreign relations). The whole basis of international law is *jurisdiction*—what actions were permitted to which governments on what territory and to which groups of people (or individuals). In turn, jurisdiction crucially depended on what was to be considered domestic and what was external. For example, people on a prince's territory were "nationals," whereas people from another ruler's territory were "aliens." International law—the law that was developed to order relations among the new states—made it clear that there were differences in what was allowed for nationals compared with aliens. A key and one of the primary functions of borders, therefore, was to *define and delineate the boundaries of states*; to delineate the areas of legal jurisdiction and to indicate which rights and responsibilities states had, and where.[1]

We know, however, that international law and legal concerns have never been key components of realism. Nevertheless, as we can now see, territoriality is a central component that defines a state. But territoriality has also long been seen as a central component of state security, because it is fundamental to the *geopolitical setting* (or context), which also affects the security of states. The territoriality of states is demarcated by the legal boundaries—or borders—that surround each state. Thus, borders are fundamental to understanding the territorial state within the realist, security-oriented, Westphalian system, and how the geopolitical context of each state is defined.

Thus, the second broad way to view borders within a realist perspective is that borders have been seen as intimately related to the security of states, which is the primary concern of realism. John Herz (1957), for example, argued that the basis for the selection of different forms of human organization was how well they could provide protection for people. The territorial state, with its sovereignty, provided a "hard shell," thus making the state the dominant form of organization. The chief thesis of Herz's classic 1957 article, "was that for centuries the characteristics of the basic political unit, the nation-state, had been its 'territoriality,' that is, its being identified with an area which, surrounded by a 'wall of defensibility,' was relatively impermeable to outside penetration and thus capable of satisfying one fundamental urge of humans—protection" (1968, 76–77). That is, the legal characteristic of sovereignty plus the large areas of territory delineated by borders provided the basis of state security.

Writing in the 1950s, Herz initially felt that the era of nuclear weapons, delivered by long-range bombers and missiles, would require that states be replaced by the "bloc," a much larger mode of organization, dominated by a single power, and the only form of organization capable of existing in a bipolar world of nuclear superpowers. In essence, Herz argued that the strategic interdependence of states (which could no longer maintain a "hard shell" against the penetration of nuclear delivery systems), would lead to the demise of the territorial state. However, a decade after his initial article Herz (1968) recanted. He recognized that the allure and power of the territorial state as a mode of organization transcended his earlier argument regarding defense, to issues of economic well-being, identity, recognition, and status.

The important point for this discussion is that for many analysts and policy makers, especially realists, the borders of states both represented, and *were,* the "hard shell" promised by the (legal) phenomenon of sovereignty. The geopolitics of the nineteenth and first half of the twentieth centuries not only stressed the immutable effects of geography, but carried much of this determinism over to the geopolitical arrangement of states as well. Where a state was located, which other states sat on its borders, and how large/small or powerful/weak they were, how long or vulnerable those borders were, and how those legal borders related to geographical features, were all key questions in the analysis of a state's security. We must also keep in mind Kenneth Boulding's concept of a "critical boundary," which captures the defensive aspects of a border, but at the same time moves away from the legal character of a border:

> The legal boundary of a nation, however, is not always its most significant boundary. We need to develop a concept of a *critical boundary,* which may be the same as the legal boundary but which may lie either inside it or outside it.... The penetration of an alien organization inside this critical boundary will produce grave disorganization.... War, therefore is only useful as a defense of the national organism if it is carried on outside the critical boundary. (1962, 265; emphasis in original)

Much of the validity in security-oriented geopolitical realist arguments remains. Whether the legal boundary or the critical boundary, borders can also serve as a clear-cut "trip wire" during militarized disputes. Moving military forces toward another state's borders is an indicator of a serious threat to a state's security and territory. Such was the case when Nasser moved Egyptian forces across the Sinai toward Israel in 1967. Elsewhere, alliances have been characterized as "manipulable" borders—as ways to overcome distance and geographic constraints and as mechanisms by which states can project capabilities beyond their own borders to newly contiguous areas. In turn, alliances have also been characterized as having a "trip-wire" function in regard to conflict, especially situations of extended, or third-party, deterrence. Such a trip-wire function, it has been argued, was the main purpose for stationing US troops in the Federal Republic of Germany during the Cold War. So, although alliances might be considered as manipulable borders, borders may play the same symbolic trip-wire functions as alliances by drawing lines that adversaries cross only at their peril.

But recall that in the "new geopolitics," geography was seen as only one of a set of conditioning factors, providing possibilities and opportunities, both facilitating and constraining choices and behavior. In addition, a set of approaches to international relations questioned realists' focus on military security and the efficacy of borders in providing a "hard shell" that states could control.

Non-Realist Approaches: Questioning the Importance of Borders

Various "liberal" or "pluralist" models of international politics have developed over the past fifty to sixty years to challenge realism. These include the development of models of *integration* (e.g., Deutsch et al. 1957; Haas 1958) that dealt with the processes by which states could create common interests and economic organizations that would promote transactions and prosperity, and that, finally, would promote the peaceful management of the political, economic, and social differences that generated conflict. In addition there were various *transnational* models or theories of international interaction (e.g., Keohane and Nye 1972, 1977), which included other actors in addition to states: international organizations (IGOs), nongovernmental organizations (NGOs, including multinational corporations, or MNCs), and ultimately broader areas of interstate cooperation known as "regimes" (see Krasner 1983; Keohane 1984). As with theories of integration, transnational theories explicitly looked at the interaction between internal factors as well as the external relations of states, and argued that military security did not always sit at the top of state interests for all states. Both looking within societies and governments and denying security primacy of importance to all states at all times violated core assumptions of realism. Economic issues, for a variety of reasons, were seen as more important for large numbers of state and non-state actors.

These approaches, and a number of others, were built around ideas of interdependence, externalities, collective goods, and the problems of collective choice (e.g., Starr 1997; Ostrom 1990). Ultimately, these approaches argued that states did better taking care of longer-term collective interests than their short-term self-interests. Only in this way could states deal with the prisoner dilemma situations that were produced by interdependence and collective goods or common pool resources (such as the "tragedy of the commons").

Along with the approaches to international relations noted previously, other models of economic interdependence (e.g.,

Kobrin 1997) as well as the current attention to globalization make an even more fundamental critique of realism: they question the existence or utility of sovereignty, territoriality, or the importance of borders in this highly interdependent, globalized world. That is, they question the utility of constraints on the movement of people, goods, or ideas in a global system that has been linked by new communication and transportation technology (again, technology changing the meaning of geography, size, and distance). They question the degree to which borders can still provide any form of "hard shell" around a state and whether they even should! Today, it is clear that technological developments in weaponry, communications, and transportation have indeed made borders far more permeable, penetrated, and porous than ever. I agree that many if not most of these claims have validity in our twenty-first-century world. Yet, analysts would be greatly mistaken to underestimate the legal importance of borders and their role in assigning jurisdiction and responsibility in the contemporary international system.

Borders in the Contemporary System: Why Should We Care?

Nevertheless, borders remain an important component of possibilism and opportunity: they both help enable and constrain the flow of people, goods, and ideas. Karl Deutsch, in discussing the elements of any social "system," included the idea of "boundaries." To discuss any social system, for example a territorial state in the global system, we must identify its boundaries. Such boundaries were important because they indicated "marked discontinuities" from one side of the boundary to the next (Deutsch 1966). Realists have looked at such discontinuities in terms of military capability and governmental control. Other approaches, which now downplay the role of borders, point out that many such discontinuities have been much reduced or have disappeared altogether. Perhaps the best example of this is the European Union, where many economic and social discontinuities have been removed. Rather than hard-shell military boundaries enforcing discontinuities, most states in the current system find that law and legal practices create these discontinuities. For example, on one side of the US-Canadian border, the patterns of tax payment show flows to Ottawa, whereas on the other side of the border, tax flows move toward Washington, DC.

Indeed, for contiguous democracies, which make up Deutschian "security communities" or zones of peace, borders are almost completely concerned with issues of legal jurisdiction regarding commerce and other economic and social transactions. Given the "democratic peace," which observes that pairs of democracies have not fought wars against each other, borders no longer are concerned with national security and survival and have far less to do with conflict/militarized conflict, than legal issues of economic jurisdiction. The previous chapter looked at spatial effects on conflict, especially contiguous borders. The non-realist approaches noted before, which stress interdependence and cooperation, democracy, and integration, look at borders in terms of how they affect cooperation, coordination, commerce, and finding answers to common problems. In that regard, borders still have an important role to play. That is, they still have an impact on interaction opportunities.

Revisiting Borders and Interaction Opportunities

Borders delineate and clarify the arrangement of the territorial units (states) that make up the international or global system. They provide vital information regarding the question of "distance" in many of its various forms: how close or far units are, in regard to security, social interaction, or economic relations. Data sets on international borders, however, have tended to measure or operationalize borders in terms of contiguous land borders—either between two states, between states and other territories, or between the colonial territorial holdings of two states. However, borders do not just refer to the contiguous land borders between two states, but also to terms of distance across bodies of water. Indeed, there is a substantial area of complex international law dealing with international borders in relation to rivers, lakes, and the sea (e.g., straits, or the continental shelf, or the width of the territorial sea).

As noted in Chapter 1, students of international relations have been concerned with distance for two broad reasons. The first is that states that are close to each other are better able to interact—the "interaction opportunity" argument or approach. One key aspect of borders is that they affect the *interaction opportunities* of states, constraining or expanding the *possibilities* of interaction that are available to them. States that share borders will tend to have a greater *ease* of interaction with one another and thus will tend to have greater numbers of interactions. Such opportunity might be measured by the *number* of other countries with which any single state has interaction opportunities. It might also be measured by the degree to which such opportunity exists between any particular pair of states. For example, Wesley (1962) argued that the length of a common border between two countries is a better measure of "geographic opportunity" than simply the number of borders. The second reason concerns willingness. States that are close to each other are perceived as important or salient to each other, for a variety of reasons. Greater perceptions of threat, gain, or interdependence are ways in which proximity can generate salience and make states more "relevant" to one another.

We have also noted that territory serves at least two distinct purposes in the study of international relations. As noted, by defining the territorial political units, borders create spatial arrangements of the units. Secondly, as the place where people live, territory provides an important component of group identity and symbolic importance as well as importance based on the resources of the territory. To repeat, territory, very simply, is important to people. It both becomes a source of conflict and raises the stakes of any conflict because of symbolic and objectively real value. *Borders—especially the contiguous land borders between two states—provide opportunities for conflict or cooperation.* Borders have an impact on the willingness of decision makers to choose certain policy options, in that they act as indicators of areas of great importance or salience.

The opportunity for interaction concept, as measured by borders and contiguity, points to the possibilities for increased interaction and the increased probability of interactions—both positive and negative. It must be stressed that interaction opportunity only holds that closer units will interact more. Borders are not simply facilitating mechanisms, however; they may also be constraining mechanisms that block interaction. The governments of Westphalian states guard their borders and police them, to allow some things/people in and to keep others out. Borders may help to create or promote a powerful we/they or us/them divide over territory, becoming both the symbol and mechanism of this divide. Borders figure significantly in conflicts over territorial claims, changes, disputes, and their settlement. Borders also figure in conflicts over the movement of people, such as foreign workers and immigrants (both legal and illegal), refugees, and those charged with crimes (both domestic and international).

The Functions and Consequences of Borders—
Legal, Political, Social, and Ethical

The Westphalian legacy emphasizes that borders delineate areas of governmental jurisdiction, and thus, *control*; that governments exercise the only legitimate authority within those borders, over the territory, people, and property within those borders. From this perspective, we also have an emphasis on how borders highlight the separateness of people/peoples, especially regarding the security aspects of the anarchic Westphalian system of self-help and the security dilemma. However, the integration perspective, especially as it entails democracies (the only successful examples of integration—Deutschian security communities, which are either amalgamated or pluralistic— involve democracies), may provide a different picture. As noted, for contiguous democracies, borders are almost completely concerned with issues of legal jurisdiction regarding transactions, especially economic ones.

However, as the place where people live, territory also provides an important component of group identity and becomes endowed with extraordinary symbolic importance to people (this is in addition to value based on resources). We have noted David Newman's notion of territory as a "demographic container" that holds people, adding territorial symbolism to their identity, with that territory becoming an "exclusive entity" for a people. Borders thus can figure significantly in conflicts over territorial claims, territorial changes, territorial disputes, and their settlement. In various works Newman summarizes a large contemporary literature in geography (and political science). Borders are no longer seen as "natural," but all borders are human constructs. Borders define territories or territoriality—they act as markers, as modes of communication, as well as control or access. As R. D. Sack (1986, 22) notes, "each instance of territoriality must involve an attempt at enforcing *control over access* to the area and to things within it, or to things outside of it by *restraining* those within" (emphasis added). This control over access has raised a variety of questions, including ethical ones, among geographers and political scientists.

David Newman (2006a, 176) notes that borders separate people in important sociological or psychological ways, in some manner creating the following sorts of distinctions: Here-There, Us-Them, Include-Exclude, Self-Other, or Inside-Outside. When added to a basic set of security and legal issues, the "management of the border regime determines the relative ease or difficulty with which borders are crossed, or alternately the extent to which the borders still constitute a barrier to movement of people, goods and ideas" (Newman 2006a, 172). Newman (e.g., 2006b) indicates two different ways by which territory and borders are being viewed—the "security discourse" and the "borderless world discourse" (strongly reflecting the globalization approach noted before). The "security discourse" deals more with how borders are used and the effects they have on the requirements of security. The "borderless world discourse" is more concerned with the nature of the governments (democratic or nondemocratic) and levels of interdependence, interaction, and integration. Newman concisely summarizes the relationship of borders and ease of interaction across them from a *non-realist* perspective:

The globalization impact on borders is as geographically and socially differentiated as most other social phenomena—in some places, it results in the opening of borders and the associated created or transition zone borderlands, while in others, the borderland remains a frontier in which mutual suspicions, mistrust of the other and a desire to maintain group or national exclusivity remain in place. This is perhaps why the opening and removal of borders in parts of Western Europe (such as between France and Germany) are all the more remarkable, given the historical realities of these conflictual and war-filled regions. (2006a, 181)

The evolution of the EU includes the especially significant 1985 Schengen Agreement(s) for the free movement of the nationals of signatory states.[2] Schengen removed cross-border barriers such as border checks and border posts and created a common visa policy for signatories. These agreements exemplify the "borderless world discourse" and the *non*security orientation of a Deutschian pluralistic security community. It is in Europe that we also find the best example of how geographers have shifted from study of a "border" or set of borders, to the *bordering process*. This is yet another example of the continuing role of borders in the study of international relations. Newman notes,

It is the process of bordering, rather than the border outcomes per se, which should be of interest to all border scholars. The process through which borders are demarcated and managed are central to the notion of border as process and border as institution.... Borders constitute institutions that enable legitimation, signification and domination, creating a system of order through which control can be exercised. Management procedures are central to this process. (2006b, 6)

By "management procedures," Newman refers to a point stressed earlier: how borders allow or prevent physical *movement and access* (see also Hyndman 2012). It is here that major ethical issues are raised. Currently, in Western Europe, with the growth of pluralistic integration through the historical evolution of the EU, we find the following bordering process: "The border is transformed from a barrier, through which the other side is invisible, to a place where reconciliation, cooperation and coexistence take place" (Newman 2006b, 4). Ethical questions arise in the process by which borders are opened or closed. Often when the security discourse and the borderless world discourse clash, as in the Mexican–US border or the fences used along the borders of Israeli and Palestinian controlled territory, the security discourse is dominant. Newman elaborates,

> While the opening of boundaries is seen as a positive factor … recent years have shown just how easily these bridges can be destroyed and the barriers reconstructed. *This raises ethical questions concerning the construction and management of boundaries—for whom, by whom, and in whose interests are some people excluded, or cut off, from their cultural, ethnic or economic living spaces?* … Good fences do not automatically create good neighbors. (2006b, 8; emphasis added)

Conclusion

Borders matter. Even in today's "turbulent," post–Cold War world of growing democracy, ever-extensive interdependence, and globalization, borders still serve a wide variety of functions across the areas of security, economics, politics, and social interactions. Even as some aspects of international law challenge or erode traditional notions of sovereignty, borders delineate areas of legal competence, perhaps more important today than ever before. Borders define the location of states and thus help provide structure to the global system, indicating which states are near or far away, or separated by oceans, rivers, or constructed lines of latitude and longitude. They have meaning for both the "security discourse" and the "borderless world discourse." They are critical to the identity of groups and how the different identities of groups separated by borders (or *not* separated by borders!) affect their social, political, or security relationships.

CHAPTER 5
ALLIANCES AND GEOPOLITICS

Combining Theory and Substance: Alliances

I have tried, in the first four chapters, to provide a variety of useful items to go into our conceptual and theoretical toolbox. With that foundation, we will now move on to the first of four applications of the ways in which geopolitical approaches can help us understand international relations and international conflict and cooperation. In this chapter the toolbox will be applied to help us understand alliances through the broader context of geopolitics and geopolitical perspectives on international relations. Using the Sprouts' ecological triad framework and the opportunity and willingness framework, alliances are viewed as part of the web of geopolitical constraints that affect possibilities in the international system. Alliances are viewed as part of the set of incentive structures that affect foreign policy decision making and as a central mechanism that permits decision makers to overcome the geopolitical constraints of the system. Drawing on analogies with technology and borders, alliances can be viewed as important tools for overcoming the constraints of geopolitics and for changing the meaning of the supposedly "permanent" nature of international geography.

Conceptualizing Alliances

Despite the many contributions that have been made to the study of international alliances, much of the research on this topic provides a clear example of the "need to reconceptualize exactly what it is that we [analysts] want to study, and why" (Most and Starr 1989, Chapter 5). Put briefly, Most and Starr elaborate a detailed argument of foreign policy substitutability, where varying conditions might lead foreign policy decision makers to substitute one foreign policy tool for another. This means that, confronted with a foreign policy situation, apparently distinct or incommensurable behaviors could be chosen. Given the situation, or context, there may be a many-to-one mapping, or a one-to-many mapping of foreign policy factors and foreign policy responses. Most and Starr also elaborate the notion of domain-specific "nice" laws, which calls for a reevaluation of the utility of searching only for the broadest general laws. Their argument is that situational, context-oriented nice laws, which do well for a specific subset of cases, are an important goal of research. These two arguments lead to the conclusion that many events have been studied in isolation, as ad hoc hypotheses, and have lost their connection to the broader concepts that are actually of concern:

> Students of international relations have, in many cases, actually reified the operational indicators of international interaction. We have studied war qua war, alliances qua alliances, and have tended to overlook the broader international processes and phenomena that such specific forms of behavior represent. (Most and Starr 1989, 107)

Our purpose here is to look at alliances within such a broader context. For many questions (but certainly not all), alliances take on meaning as part of the geopolitical context of international relations. By explicitly presenting alliances within a geopolitical context (or any broader theoretical context), I hope to make the work on alliance more complete. Most work on alliance does not explicitly or systematically take geopolitics into account; much of the work on geopolitics does not explicitly or systematically deal with alliances. Indeed, within the broader concern for cumulation of international relations theory and findings, the lack of cumulation in the study of alliances came in for specific critical comment in the 1980s (e.g., see Job 1981; Ward 1982). Given that alliances have been studied in terms of their formation, duration, and disintegration, and their specific relation to war—rather than as possible mechanisms in processes of social cooperation, coordination, and integration, or as part of general security concerns and calculations—the lack of cumulation is not surprising. Alliances need to be reconceptualized in terms of what they "really" represent for particular research questions—of which larger concepts they are examples. Given that foreign policy mechanisms or behavior can substitute for one another, we need to step back and ask what alliances are about before we design research to study them or use them as indicators in our studies.

Clearly, one very important perspective on alliances is geopolitics. Alliances can take on meaning, in the context urged by Most and Starr, by thinking of them within a broader environmental or "ecological" context. Alliances can be seen as an important component of the Sprouts' ecological triad— as an entity for some questions, as an environment for other questions, as a linkage in the entity-environment relationship for yet other questions. Although the Sprouts' ideas were conceptually rich, at the same time they were relatively lacking in the empirical specificity necessary for use in empirical research. I tried to find ways to overcome this problem by developing the ideas of opportunity and willingness. If we are indeed concerned with how alliances affect the structure of the international environment, as well as the calculations made by foreign policy actors within that environment, we are thus concerned with how alliances affect and reflect the opportunity and willingness of states.

Using my broader version of the Sprouts' ecological triad, and especially the use of opportunity, alliances become part of the international system's structure of possibilities/constraints. Additionally, alliances might also be seen as the means by which states deal or cope with the physical possibilities or constraints presented by geography. We have argued Giddens's (1984, 169) view that structure is "always both enabling and constraining." Alliances, as international structures, have both effects.

As long as there are possibilities, there is room for choice. Although some choices will be more likely than others, the basic notion is that choice is based on probability calculations. Alliances, as part of the configuration of environmental structures, thus also affect the decision calculi of policy makers. Alliances can be seen as important components of the incentive structures available for states. They are relevant to the choices to be made by decision makers by affecting the perceptions of decision makers as to how costly or risky certain options appear to be. Alliances comprise, in part, the structure of risks and opportunities that confront decision makers. And as we have seen earlier, the Sprouts' cognitive behaviorism and its brief reference to the psycho-milieu of policy makers only begin to touch on the complexity of the relationship between place and image. Thus, alliances as part of the international incentive structure may affect the willingness of decision makers in their foreign policy choices. But the decision to enter into an alliance itself reflects a willingness to accept the potential costs of alliance as balanced against potential gains. Alliances may be seen as conscious choices of decision makers that indicate positions of policy preference. The formal commitments indicated by alliances demonstrate a willingness to align policy with certain states rather than others; they indicate a willingness to side with some states rather than others. This willingness to extend a state's commitments also feeds back and becomes part of the total set of incentive structures that each state must work within. In this way alliances reflect the complex relationship between opportunity and willingness.[1]

As an aside, I discovered that a reconceptualization of alliances as a factor related explicitly to both opportunity and willingness within a broader geopolitical view of international relations was necessary to develop, focus, and ground the empirical study of alliances, diffusion, and international conflict, as was done in Siverson and Starr (1991). To show how these purposes were achieved, we see how alliances might fit within the geopolitical perspective developed so far in this book. I will expand on the relationship between alliances and the concept of opportunity and follow with a section on alliances and willingness. A final concluding section will comment on the study of alliance and diffusion.

The Place of Alliances in Geopolitics

In a useful review of several major treatments of the topic of geopolitics, Østerud (1988) notes the heterogeneous usage of the term and the variety of meanings it has taken on. He is particularly critical of usages that are either ideological or highly deterministic. He then asserts that, "'Geopolitics' is not a term for the general linkage of politics to geography. It should rather be understood as a conceptual and terminological tradition in the study of the political and strategic relevance of geography" (1988, 191). Although we are not concerned with all possible connections between geography and political phenomena in this chapter, we could propose that alliances broadly relate to both the "functional organization of space" and the "formal organization of space" (Berry 1969)—that is, both relative distance as well as absolute distance. Location and topography reflect both notions of distance. Harold Sprout (1963, 192) once asserted that all geopolitical hypotheses "represent assessments of opportunities and limitations implicit in the milieu of the interacting nations." He claimed that all such hypotheses fit into either of two categories: those derived mainly (though never exclusively) from the layout and configuration of lands and seas, regional variations of climate, or uneven distribution of minerals and other earth materials; and those derived from the distribution of people or some set of social institutions or other behavioral patterns. Both categories reflect the complexity of location and distance set out in Chapter 2.

Some students of geopolitics have taken this basic position and placed it within a highly realist view of international politics. The geographer Saul Cohen (1963, 24), for example, notes that, "The essence of geopolitical analysis is the relation of international power to the geopolitical setting." G. R. Sloan (1988, viii) has argued that geopolitical theory connects geography and political history and is a theory of "spatial relationships and historical causation." Alliances are clearly related to the aggregation of the military capabilities of others to one's own capabilities, or to the denial of the military capabilities of others to one's opponents. In large part this is owing to the absolute location of the military capabilities of one's allies and one's opponents. It is also because of relative distance: how quickly and with what cost those capabilities could be "projected" or moved. In all these ways we cannot escape the inclusion of realist conceptions of power in the linkages between alliance and geopolitics.

In this book, we have stressed geopolitical phenomena as being important components of the context of international relations. As with the Sprouts, the geographer John O'Loughlin (1987, 2) sees one potential contribution of political geography as "the accurate identification and mapping of the meaningful contexts for the actors engaged in interstate relations," including not only those contexts that immediately surround states but also those that "will vary from the substate through hemispheric to global scales." By thinking of environments and the entities within them, and how the entities perceive the environment, we are not locked into any specific factor (such as geography) or level of analysis, thus partially avoiding the false micro/macro distinction Giddens (1984) warns against. The opportunity-willingness framework leads us to a conception of context analogous to Giddens's concept of "locale" (1984). We also see the impact of substitutability and nice laws by recognizing that context is situationally differentiated and dynamic.[2] Context is not static. Even in our concern with geography as one component of the international/geopolitical context, the mapping process is to be seen as a dynamic in which space is a contingent factor, where territoriality is constantly in motion. Thus, the ideographic reification of specific places or spaces is avoided. Put simply, there is a constant dynamic in the configuration and reconfiguration of space within the context of international relations—with alliances as an important mechanism of this dynamic.

Within the geographical component of the environment's structure of constraints and possibilities, alliances have an important role to play. As consciously manipulable indicators of policy preference, they can and do change, and in so doing, change the spatial relationships among friends and opponents: how close they might be; how their relative military capabilities stand in relationship to one another (e.g., the loss-of-strength gradient); or, how alliances might "substitute" for borders by altering the configurations of interaction opportunities (see Starr and Most 1976; Siverson and Starr 1991). Many contextual aspects of geopolitics, including the effects of relative space and time-space, can be applied to alliances and their effects on international relations. This can be shown by looking at Harold Sprout's two groups of geopolitical hypotheses. The first looks at the physical constraints of geography—or opportunity. In what follows, we will discuss the ability of alliances to leapfrog distance and topography.

Sprout's second group of hypotheses is concerned with the social and political configurations of humans in space. From a realist point of view, this is exactly what alliances are about when we think in terms of alliances and the balance of power. But the Sproutian idea is much broader. Alliances *change* the political configuration of the international system. They alter, often quite rapidly and unexpectedly, the politically relevant boundaries. They give new meaning to the political boundaries that are drawn on maps. Alliances thus become central to the geopolitical distribution of political preferences/coalitions/calculations in the international system. This is why I noted in Chapter 1 that Colin Gray's observation about geographical permanence only tells part of the story. The creation, dissolution, or growth of alliances—as social institutions—is clearly one source of change in the international geopolitical structure.

Alliances and Opportunity

As an important component of the structure of the international system, alliances change the interaction opportunities available to states. Alliances are thus central to the geopolitical structure that constrains states, but simultaneously act as mechanisms by which that geopolitical structure and its incentive structures might be changed. Alliances can clearly be described in terms of interaction opportunities (e.g., Siverson and Starr 1991). The conceptual linkage between borders and alliances is easily shown. Although a state's borders are not readily manipulable by policy makers, its alliances are. We can, then, interpret alliance formations (and dissolutions) as attempts by policy makers to alter their border-related risks and opportunities—or, in other words, as efforts to create or destroy borders. When two contiguous states ally in a mutual defense pact, for example, they may in a sense be "removing" (or at least decreasing the importance of) their common border. Alternatively, as a state loses the real borders it once had through its colonial possessions, it may have attempted to retain its access and control and legitimize its activity in various regions by creating "pseudo-borders," that is those created by alliances. In that sense, military and economic alliances may have been substituted for colonial empires in the post–World War II period.

If alliances can be used to indicate the salience and importance of states to one another and delineate subgroups of highly interacting states, then they should have an impact on the diffusion of war similar to that found in studies using borders as "agents" of diffusion. I have investigated this (with both Most and Siverson) in studies that have compared borders, alliances, and their combined interactive effects on the diffusion of war. These studies looked at both major powers and all states across the 1816–1965 period.[3] These studies also looked at two different forms of diffusion as well as a general relationship between border or alliance interaction opportunities and war. We found that whereas both borders and alliances have significant effects on the spread or occurrence of war, the effects of diffusion (or the overall proclivity to war) appear to be *generally stronger for alliances* than for borders. However, the *combination* of alliance and border effects (for example, having a partner in a defensive alliance that also shares a contiguous land border) generally improves on using either alone. Also the more extensive the effects (that is, the larger the number of bordering states or alliance partners at war or involved in the ongoing war), the greater the interaction opportunity effect. In addition, the strength of the results were found to scale roughly from the strongest to weakest indicators of opportunity (for borders the strongest results derive from contiguous homeland borders, and the weakest from colonial borders) and from the strongest to weakest indicators of policy willingness (for alliances the strongest results derive from defense pacts, and the weakest from ententes).

In sum, the interaction opportunity model was found to perform impressively across different research designs. Alliances, as part of the geopolitical structure of interaction opportunities, did act as an important mechanism by which wars were found to occur and spread. The analysis of alliance as an aspect of opportunity can also be expanded to cover a variety of alliance studies. If one reason that states form alliances is to project capabilities, as well as aggregate capabilities, then alliances are involved in the extension of a state's ability to interact militarily with other actors. This conception of alliances is thus closely related to the loss-of-strength gradient. If states are concerned with security or military viability vis-à-vis other states as part of their environmental context, they must be concerned with the physical ability, or possibility, that other states bring military capabilities to bear upon them. We have discussed this as part of relative distance in its various forms: What absolute distance must such military capability cross, and what physical barriers stand in its way? The formation of alliances to project capability is thus one mechanism by which states may overcome the geopolitical constraints of distance and topographical features.

Stephen Walt (1985) deals indirectly with alliances as mechanisms to extend states' military interaction opportunities. His discussion of alternative models to explain why states join great power alliances is based, in part, on the *level of threat* that states face. In essence, Walt's argument is that states ally with others on the basis of threat and not power. He indicates four factors that affect the level of threat: aggregate power, proximity, offensive capability, and offensive intentions. By combining Walt's factors of proximity and offensive capability, alliances increase threat to outside parties bordering the alliance partners, and do so by overcoming distance and physical barriers, by creating new geopolitical realities. As Walt notes (1985, 10–11), proximate threats can generate either checkerboard effects (under a balancing response) or a sphere-of-influence effect (under a "bandwagoning" response). Either way, the use of alliances to project capability creates threat that reconfigures the geopolitical distribution of power and political allegiance. If we look closely at proximity and threat, we see states (usually major powers) in a dynamic of expanding their defensive or offensive spheres (aggregating military capability, projecting military capability, or attempting to forestall the opponent from doing either). The interaction opportunities created by new alliance networks allow formerly distant states to be proximate, hence to interact, and thus raise the probability of conflictual interaction.

Such alliance dynamics may create "intersections" similar to those described in Choucri and North's (1975) lateral-pressure model. They argue that as the factors of population and technology create greater demands for resources, states expand (in various ways) to acquire the needed resources. The expansion of spheres or areas of control will inevitably come into contact, increasing the probability of conflict. Choucri and North (1975, 25) outline the components of their conceptual model as follows:

- Expansion: Demands resulting from the interactive effects of population and technological growth give rise to activities beyond national borders.
- Conflict of interest: Expanding nations are likely to collide in their activities outside national boundaries; such collisions have some potential for violence.
- Military capability: States, by definition, have military establishments; these grow as the result of domestic growth and competition with military establishments of other nations.
- Alliance: Nations assess their power, resources, and capabilities in comparison with other nations and attempt to enhance themselves through international alliances.
- Violence-behavior: Nations engage in international violence as a consequence of expansion, military capability, and alliances.

Alliances, then, are a key component to the Choucri and North lateral-pressure model as well as a separate source of intersections. Although Choucri and North do not treat it as such, it is clear that their model is essentially a geopolitical one, as it rests on the spatial expansion of the colonial, economic, and resource spheres of states. In their model the intensity of intersections is positively related to alliances, as are military expenditures. Alliances, in turn, are positively related to violent behavior. Choucri and North's concept of intersection appears to be similar to O'Sullivan's (1986) concern with the "intersection of force fields," where conflict will occur due to uncertainty. We can interpret this as deriving from the collision or intersection of spheres/capabilities at some distance from each state and the *lack of clarity* over the effects of the loss-of-strength gradient in any such situation. So, alliances allow the projection of capabilities and are used to facilitate the expansion of spheres of influence or control. These sorts of effects can be fully conceptualized in geopolitical terms.

Another, and even more direct, concern with interaction opportunity relates to conflicts that arise over territory. We have noted Diehl's views on territory. Territory was not only a "facilitating" condition, but also a source of conflict. Diehl then asks *when* will states go to war over some territory, and what characteristics will make some territory worth fighting over? One answer to Diehl's questions again relates directly to alliances. In 1915, James Fairgrieve developed the concept of the "crush zone," described as "the belt of small countries lying between the heartland and the sea powers" (O'Sullivan 1986, 33). A crush zone could be seen as a buffer zone, and also as territory to be fought over, as Diehl suggests. What is not explicitly recognized in the literature, however, is that during the Cold War, the competing blocs of alliances absorbed much of what composed the crush zones. Cohen (1963, 83) updated Fairgrieve's concept with his own conception of the "shatterbelt," which is a "large, strategically located region that is occupied by a number of conflicting states and is caught between conflicting interests of Great Powers." It, too, constitutes the sort of territory that states fight over. One could think of post–World War II relations between the Western and Eastern blocs and the use of alliances (primarily by the West) as a way both to leapfrog buffer zones and to project Western capability beyond those areas Cohen calls shatterbelts. This, in effect, constituted the strategy of containment and encirclement of the Eisenhower administration, and particularly Eisenhower's secretary of state, John Foster Dulles.

In sum, regarding interaction opportunities, alliances can be used to overcome distance and topographical constraints, and importantly—time. In so doing, they foster proximity and project capabilities. By Walt's argument, this creates threat. Although threat would be enhanced by ideological factors (to which Walt devotes considerable attention), the geopolitical factors of proximity and the ability to project military capability would appear to be primary bases of threat.

Alliances as Instruments of Adaptation

Conceiving of existing alliances as interaction opportunities is only one form of opportunity derived from possibilism or probabilism. Alliances may also be conceptualized as one mechanism decision makers may use to cope with or "adapt" to that environment. We can use James Rosenau's discussion of adaptation (e.g., 1980) as one perspective by which to link entities to their environments. Rosenau comes close to some of the Sproutian entity-environment notions by noting,

"Considerable insight follows from an initial formulation that conceives national societies—like the single cell, the individual, group, or organization—as entities that must adapt to their environments to survive and prosper" (1980, 503).

If alliances are used to cope with distance or the military capability of proximate or distant states, or to restructure the incentive structures of alliances, enemies, or nonaligned states, then alliances are adaptation mechanisms. As Rosenau notes, "Any external behavior undertaken by the government of any national society is adaptive when it copes with, or stimulates, changes in its external environment that contribute to keeping its essential structures within acceptable limits" (1980, 503).

A useful analogy is between alliances and technology, which both overcome the effects of geography. One of the primary reasons that the geographical/topographical constraints that face states are not "permanent" is that they have regularly been overcome or modified by technological innovation in transportation, communication, and military weaponry. Indeed, the revolution in international politics that was seen with the advent of nuclear weapons relies just as heavily (or more) upon the technological developments in delivery systems. It is the existence of these delivery systems that has negated the traditional effects of distance and space, and of topographical physical barriers such as oceans. Thus, during the Cold War era of ICBMs, the United States gained no advantage from its ocean barriers, nor did the Soviet Union reap the same benefit from its vast expanses as it did under the czars or during World War II.

Harold Sprout argued convincingly (1963, 194) that, although the pioneering geopoliticians Sir Halford Mackinder (who focused on land power and the "Heartland" theory) and Alfred Thayer Mahan (who focused on naval forces and "sea power") both looked at the same geographical reality, their conclusions differed "because of the different weights that each assigned to the properties and significance of advancing technology." Sprout holds that Mahan's view faltered because he failed to pay attention to technological innovation and its effect on the relationship between military capabilities and geography: "Mahan, like so many of his contemporaries, seems to have taken it for granted that the future would not be very different from the immediate past" (1963, 194–195). Previously we noted that alliances can leapfrog distance and geography. By so doing, alliances also change the meaning of distance, space, and the physical arrangements of the earth's features. But alliances have the advantage of not being dependent on the serendipity of scientific/technological breakthroughs (and the translation of such advances into military, political, or economic instruments). Just as we may conceive of alliances as manipulable borders, alliances may also be conceived of as "political technology." The rapid projection of military capability through diplomacy and treaty formation can render former geopolitical realities meaningless by changing not only the *absolute* distance between units, but their time–distance as well. State A, which does not have a contiguous border with State B, is now able to border State B through an alliance with State C, which *is* contiguous to B. This exact issue arose among NATO, Turkey, and Iraq prior to and immediately after the onset of the second Gulf War, given the desire of the United States to reduce the loss-of-strength gradient of bringing military force to bear on Iraq.

Although the second Gulf War is the most recent example, many other important historic examples could be cited. Two examples of attempts to create anti-US alliances may indicate how important such foreign policy activities have been to US policy makers. The German attempt, however feeble, to form some type of political/military coalition with Mexico prior to the United States' entry into World War I demonstrates the perception that alliance can be used to overcome physical boundaries. The impact of this attempted alliance on US willingness to enter the war indicated how serious a threat this attempt was perceived to be (as Walt would argue). The Soviet alignment with Cuba subsequent to the Cuban revolution had very similar aims and reactions, especially during the 1960s. The attempt to use a form of alliance to permit the projection of military capability and overcome geography, and the threat it created, is well reflected in all the accounts of the 1962 Cuban missile crisis.

In sum, alliances are similar to technology as a mechanism to overcome geopolitical constraints, and as a way to alter the menu of incentives, costs, and benefits that exists in the international system. The key difference, of course, is that alliances are the result of conscious choice through diplomatic activity. Alliances are more manipulable than borders; alliances are more predictable and reliable than technological change. Decision makers are thus *willing* to create alliances, to honor alliances (or give them up), and willing to accept the geopolitical consequences of their creation. All of these actions depend on the cost-benefit-risk calculations of policy makers. Therefore, alliances include another source of dynamics—perceptions that result in changes in willingness.

Alliances and Willingness

We can outline two general relationships between alliances and willingness within a geopolitical context. The first derives from the broad question of why states are willing to enter alliances in the first place. Joining an alliance entails the potential of great risks as well as benefits. Any decision that indicates the willingness to enter an alliance indicates that the joining state expects greater benefits than costs (at least in the short run!). That is, the expected utility derived from joining the alliance is greater than that of foregoing the alliance possibility. Why do states enter alliances? Walt (1985) focuses primarily on alliance formation as a response to threat—that states balance or bandwagon with others as a mechanism for dealing with their perceptions of external threat. Although a number of the reasons why states form alliances are directly related to capabilities and security issues (and thus directly or indirectly to threat), other reasons cannot be so clearly connected. One central reason why states form alliances, and the primary reason for realists, is for the aggregation of military capability. States also seek allies in order to "preempt" these states from joining the alliances of others—that is, to keep their military capabilities from one's opponents. States may form alliances in order to take advantage of the strategic position of the ally. Whereas the first two reasons are concerned with the addition (or subtraction) of overall military capabilities, this last reason is directly related to adapting to the geopolitical environment.

Alliances may also be formed to meet a deterrent or balancing function. Alliances may add precision to state relations, and thus make a deterrent threat clearer (and more credible). The aggregation of the military capabilities of several states may also make deterrent threats more credible. Credibility may be enhanced by the projection of military capability, if that capability can serve as a "trip wire" that will serve to trigger extended deterrence. Thus, the projection of power permitted by alliances may serve aggressive or defensive functions and have threatening or provocative consequences or deterrent consequences.[4] Alliances also entail risks—that the deterrent threat will be challenged, that the alliance will drag a partner into conflicts it would prefer to ignore (with World War I the classic example), that rash or obstreperous alliance partners will create situations that will involve other alliance members (again World War I). In essence, alliances can serve as conduits along which conflict may flow. Alliances create commitments that states may be called upon to honor, with a failure to do so involving a loss of credibility.

If we are concerned with why states are willing to join alliances, we have a wide range of possible answers. For many states, however, the risks of alliance are taken because they are offset by the military/security benefits alliances seem to provide. The risks are accepted because of the opportunities that alliances provide to override the geopolitical constraints of the international system. Balancing, bandwagoning, aggregating capabilities, and projecting capabilities all provide such opportunities. A large literature using formal models on the choices made in forming alliances and meeting alliances' commitments has been built around expected utility and cost-benefit models (see, for example, Snyder 1984; Nicholson 1989; and Leeds 2003).

Conclusion

Decision makers have been willing to use alliances to overcome the constraints of geopolitics; they have been willing to accept the risks that alliances, as interaction opportunities, bring. They have been willing because those opportunities also hold many potential benefits. They have been willing because, as alliances indicate important policy congruencies between the partners, they indicate that partners may have greater salience to each other that is worth the risks of conflict with third parties.

We have looked at how alliances affect, and are related to, both opportunity and willingness, and how those relationships are embedded in geopolitical and spatial factors. The GIS-based research application in the next chapter attempts to elaborate on ways to measure the "nature" of borders in terms of opportunity and willingness.

CHAPTER 6
GEOGRAPHIC TOOLS
GEOGRAPHIC INFORMATION SYSTEMS APPLIED TO INTERNATIONAL POLITICS

Conceptualizing (and Reconceptualizing) Borders

In previous chapters GIS (geographic information systems) has been discussed as a major component of much of the newer work in geopolitics. In Chapter 1, I noted that I have used GIS as a way to help reconceptualize borders, and thus proximity and distance as well. Because a central feature of much of the geopolitical work discussed so far has been a focus on the nature and effects of spatial proximity as operationalized by international borders, a major aim of my GIS-based project can be seen as a concept-clarification exercise—to revise and reconceptualize how we think about borders and how they should be measured.

Our discussions have clearly established that a key dimension for students of geopolitics is *proximity*. We have seen that my own diffusion research moved to the study of borders after concluding that the diffusion of certain phenomena could only be studied by looking at units that were "relevant" to one another—and that such relevance could be indicated by geographical proximity. Proximity, in turn, could be operationalized through borders, because they had important relationships to both the opportunity and willingness of international actors. One key aspect of borders is that they affect the *interaction opportunities* of states; states sharing borders tend to have a greater *ease* of interaction with one another and thus will tend to have a greater number of interactions.

The opportunity for interaction has been measured most often in terms of the *number* of other countries with which any single state has borders. Other measures include the length of a common border between two countries. Wesley (1962) argued that length is a better measure of "geographic opportunity" than the number of borders; see also the more recent work of Brochmann et al. (2012) on border length and low-intensity conflict. Presaging the GIS discussion in this chapter, Wesley also suggested that length should be measured not in "actual physical length" but in terms of population units. I have argued that the opportunities-for-interaction view of borders gets at the important conceptual core of proximity in a way that other measures of distance used by international relations scholars do not. Such measures have included, for example, the use of the air mileage between the capitals of states to measure distance (Garnham 1976; Gleditsch and Singer 1975). One purpose of the GIS project presented here is to test the utility of such different conceptions of proximity as interaction opportunities. And, as has been argued, borders also have an impact on the willingness of decision makers in that they act as indicators of *areas of great importance or salience*. Because other states are close, having greater ease of interaction and the ability to bring military capabilities to bear, they are also key areas of external cues (or diffusion). Accordingly, activities in these areas are particularly worrisome, can create uncertainty, and thus deserve attention.[1]

In my work with Benjamin Most, we were also particularly concerned with the roles that different types of borders appear to play in war involvement, because different types of borders might have differential impacts on opportunity and willingness. Thus, in Starr and Most (1976) borders were differentiated in terms of homeland borders and borders generated by colonial territories. This differentiation allowed the testing of whether all territory was seen as equally important, or whether homeland territory generated greater willingness than more distantly held colonial/imperial territories. Implicitly tested in such analyses was the notion that it was homeland territory per se that was important: that the proximity of *any* homeland territory of one state to *any* homeland territory of another state was the important factor. Although some of our diffusion analyses indicated that this was probably the case, other analyses also demonstrated the strong impact of colonial territorial borders on the diffusion of war. Simply, colonial territories were responsible for creating a greater number of *opportunities* for conflictual interaction (in a way that complemented Choucri and North's model of lateral-pressure "intersections"). Our analyses also distinguished between land-based contiguity and across-water proximity. Again, such a distinction *implicitly* dealt with possible variations in ease of interaction and salience.

The GIS project described in what follows built upon the idea that borders were indicators of proximity. The use of GIS permits a much fuller and clearer specification of borders by allowing us to talk about the *specific qualities* of borders in terms of opportunity and willingness. The reconceptualization will permit us to go beyond simply observing the number of borders a state possesses, whether a border existed between two states, or the length of that border.

Methodology: ARC/INFO and the Conceptualization and Operationalization of Borders

Geographic information systems, developed through the early to mid-1960s, are now the focus of a large amount of literature produced by geographers and regional scientists (as well as political scientists). It is not my intent to review that literature here or cite the most recent contributions to it. As could be expected, there are many approaches to, and perspectives on, GIS. It is important, however, to understand that a GIS is a *tool,* founded on a variety of computer technologies, that permits the integration of data about the spatiality of phenomena along with data about other characteristics of those phenomena.

It is important to note that GIS is more than mere computer mapping. According to D. F. Marble (1990, 10), to be considered a true GIS, a system must include the following four major components: (a) a data input subsystem that collects or processes spatial data derived from existing maps, remote sensors, and so on; (b) a data storage and retrieval subsystem that organizes the spatial data in a form that permits it to be quickly retrieved by the user for subsequent analysis; (c) a data manipulation and analysis subsystem that performs a variety of tasks such as changing the form of the data through user-defined aggregation rules or producing estimates of parameters and constraints, and (d) a data reporting subsystem that is capable of displaying all or part of the original database as well as manipulated data and the output from spatial models in tabular or map form. David Cowen (1990, 57) argues that the heart of a GIS system is its ability to overlay various layers or coverages of data so that the GIS would have, "*created new information* rather than just have retrieved previously encoded information" (emphasis added). The reconceptualization of borders using GIS derives from the ability to generate new measures—or new information—about the nature of borders.

Conflict Analysis Using GIS

GIS systems have been central to a number of recent studies of interstate and intrastate conflict. For example, using GIS to analyze location, political scientists have studied the diffusion of conflict (e.g., Braithwaite 2006). Alex Braithwaite (2005) also uses GIS to study both external and internal conflict in uncovering the location of conflict "hot spots," noting that GIS was used to store, visualize, and manipulate locational data. GIS has been used to address other conflict-related questions beyond the location and diffusion of interstate conflict. For example, Starr and Thomas (2002, 2005) retest hypotheses on the relationships between territory and crises, and territory as a cause of conflict (see the following chapter). W. Wood (2000) looks at GIS as a tool for territorial negotiations. D. Gibler (2007) uses GIS-generated data to look at the interrelationships among democracy, peace, and territorial issues. K. Furlong et al. (2006) have studied conflicts and their resolution over shared rivers. For internal conflict, scholars have used a number of GIS-based data developed at the Peace Research Institute Oslo (PRIO), including the Armed Conflict Location and Event Dataset (ACLED) and the Conflict Sites polygon data (e.g., Buhaug et al. 2009; Raleigh et al. 2010; Hallberg 2012), studying the location of conflict in relation to the location of capital cities, government strongholds, physical features such as mountains, and so on. For an overview of GIS applications, see Kristian Gleditsch and Nils Weidmann (2012).

ARC/INFO and the Study of Borders[2]

The GIS system that was used in this study is ARC/INFO, developed and supplied by Environmental Systems Research Institute, Inc. (ESRI). The strengths of the version I used (first developed in the late 1990s) reside in part in its ability to integrate many kinds of data, as well as "an open architecture which allows it to be linked to a number of relational database management systems" (Peuquet and Marble 1990, 91). ARC/INFO employs a "georelational" approach, which abstracts "geographic information into a series of independently defined layers or coverages, each representing a selected set of closely associated geographic features (e.g., roads, streams, and forest stands)" (ESRI 1992, 14).[3] The large-scale database consists of sixteen layers of data. These layers contain data ranging from physical characteristics, such as drainage networks, hypsography (elevation and topographic relief), and land cover, to man-made features such as road networks, railroad networks, and aeronautical data.[4]

The GIS methodology, however, must be driven by theoretical considerations. The various layers of the ARC/INFO GIS contain a great number of variables, and the key question must be *which* of these variables should be selected to create valid indexes to represent opportunity and willingness (ease of interaction and salience). There is a large literature on the nature of boundaries produced by geographers (and by geopoliticians writing earlier this century). This literature often focuses on the meaning of boundaries for group formation, group identity, and group maintenance (see Falah and Newman 1995, as well as such seminal works as Prescott 1987 and Glassner 1992). As we have noted, the mere existence of a border can tell us many things and generate research hypotheses.

Yet, "a border is not a border is not a border." As we have seen, borders serve many functions and obviously take on different meanings in different specific contexts. No single operationalization of border, and no data set based on such an operationalization, will be able to provide the total historical-political context for all pairs of states. Nevertheless, drawing on two decades of attention to these ideas, the argument here is that the opportunity and willingness conceptualization does tap key elements of the proximity-border concept and constitutes a progressive step in the more general conceptualization of borders, context, and the analysis of international interaction.

Opportunity (Ease of Interaction)

Regarding opportunity, the variable selection decisions were based on the theoretical considerations presented in previous chapters. The notion of ease of interaction derives from Boulding's "loss-of-strength gradient," and the ability to project conventional military power. Out of the welter of possible variables (and taking various technical/analytic constraints into account), three central factors for the movement of land-based military capability were selected—the existence of roads and railroads and the steepness of terrain. This project draws from Wesley (1962), who suggests that scholars should use cross-border roads to operationalize geographic opportunity. Indeed, Bubalo and Cook (2010) have argued that development, cooperation, and "mutual relevance" in Asia is best captured not by maritime interactions but by *new roads and railways* (among other phenomena). Douglas Lemke (1995), using Bruce Bueno de Mesquita's (1981) operationalization of the loss-of-strength gradient, is also concerned with the distance over which military forces can move in specific periods of time and how this relates to the propensity for wars or militarized interstate disputes (MIDs). Lemke is specifically concerned with paved roads and railroads in attempting to estimate the loss-of-strength gradient and those countries that make up "relevant" dyads/ neighborhoods for African states.

Based on such work, an index created from these three factors both reflects ease of interaction and is applicable (that is, valid) across a large set of international dyadic boundaries. Using data available in the Digital Chart of the World's (DCW) data layers, an index was constructed that aggregates values generated from ARC/INFO. It can be used to characterize *any* border or *border segment* on the globe. After reviewing all the variables within all of the layers, the following were selected to create an "ease of interaction" index. The first variable looked for the presence or absence of roads within the locations being studied. Roads included multilane divided roads as well as primary and secondary roads. The second variable was the presence or absence of railroads. The third variable involved the slope of an area (or hypsography), which was based on the elevation values of contour lines (in mean feet above sea level) and was derived from a digital terrain model by converting the hypsography into a triangulated irregular network. Each of these values was investigated for a *buffer* area of 10,000 meters on each side of all international borders.[5]

A methodology was developed that used vector data. The results were used to create *color maps* for the opportunity for interaction. Such a map for Israel can be found in Starr's article in *Political Geography* (2002a). Readers are also directed to the web page for this book, where a link to this map may be found: **www.paradigmpublishers.com/Books/BookDetail .aspx?productID=356911.** With this methodology, I could simply note the presence or absence of roads and railroads. The hypsography, or slope, was represented as follows: coded 1 if the slope was 0°–5°, coded 2 if the slope was 6°–20°, and coded 3 if it was greater than 20°. This created a simple 1–4 index combining roads, railroads, and hypsography, with 4 (red in the color maps) representing the *greatest* ease of interaction and 1 (dark green in the color maps) the most difficult areas to move across. Note that the procedures described here were specifically developed to generate a *four*-category scheme.[6] In part, this was done to facilitate the translation of results into clear color maps (and possibly into black and white representations). Although maps are an important medium for the *presentation* of results, it must be stressed that any section of any border could now be represented by a value from 1 to 4: values that can be used in data analyses within the GIS, both with other GIS variables or any other data sets that are imported into the ARC/INFO GIS. Such a data set will be described in what follows.

When one looks at the color maps—for example the color maps of Israel on the *On Geopolitics* web page—it is easy to see the important point just noted. They clearly demonstrate that the ease of interaction *can vary* along any single border that a state might have with a contiguous neighbor (the values, as represented by different colors, vary). The opportunity for interaction variable can be used to indicate this variation along any single border (for example, Israel's border with Lebanon). This would capture the variation that might occur on a very long border—*any* particular portion of a border can thus be characterized as to its degree of permeability. Thus, we are now able to go beyond the simple idea that in some way contiguity provides the possibility for interaction—although some parts of some borders would make this highly likely or possible, other parts would make interaction much less likely. We could make

such judgments regardless of the length of a border or the number
of different borders that a state might have.

Willingness (Salience)

The salience dimension of proximity/borders is concerned with
the importance or value of territory along or behind a border.
Again, the question is how importance or value is to be measured.
Later in this chapter I will discuss an alternative hypothesis that
it is territory per se that is important. However, here we must
be concerned with indicators that would discriminate the level
of value or concern over territory (as Most and Starr [1980] did
by differentiating between homeland territory and colonial possessions, and between contiguous land borders and across-water
borders). Drawing once more on geographers, demographics
are seen as important: the territory on which a state's population lives. This was to be operationalized by areas of population
concentration. A capital city, the locus of governmental activity and the symbol of the state, should also be used to indicate
the importance of territory. Although I disagree that distance
between capital cities should be considered a primary indicator
of proximity, studies using this measure do highlight the central
importance of capital cities. Note that in selecting areas of population concentration and the seats of government we have now
captured all three of the central elements of the Westphalian state
found in the international relations literature: territory, population, and government. Areas of urban concentration, including
both urbanized areas and capital cities, were extracted from the
ARC/INFO Populated Place Layer.

Other coverages provided the location of items that would
indicate the importance of an area. For instance, from Layer

13, the Aeronautical Layer, active civil and military airports were identified. The Cultural Landmark Layer (Layer 14) provides a catalogue of items including military camps, forts, oil wells and refineries, power plants of various kinds, water tanks, factories, industrial complexes, hospitals, telecommunications stations, and so on. The wide variety of items found in Layer 14 was used because the *substantive* importance of any single type of installation could vary considerably across states. By identifying the location of key aspects of a state's transportation, communication, energy production, industrial, agricultural, and security infrastructures, we have items that tap "importance" in a manner generally relevant to all states. Note that these elements are those that can be captured by satellite imaging—and do not include assets/qualities that also make a territory important, such as subterranean resources, the ethnicity of the population, or the historical symbolism of the area. However, as noted in the discussion of GIS, any such data could be imported into the GIS analytic system.

The salience index was developed in much the same fashion as the index for opportunity for interaction. After reviewing the various coverages, the salience or importance of a border area was determined by places of population concentration, state capitals, airfields, and selected cultural features located within a 50,000-meter buffer of the region's borders. One rule that was used was that a capital city was automatically coded with the highest value found in any of the units of analysis. This vector approach to salience looked for the number of other features that were within four kilometers of any feature selected. These were then mapped based on the value, showing where clusters of features arose. The results of these analyses can be found in the color map of the salience of Israel's borders found on the book's web page.

The map displays the *clustering* of point coverages that indicate the importance of an area, with the graphics representing the numbers of points that overlap within four-kilometer ranges. Again, although the data-generating strengths of GIS have been stressed, it would be useful here to emphasize as well the *visual* utility of GIS—its ability to generate maps that help investigators look at data differently and provide heuristics for generating hypotheses and model specification.

Yet, although color map representations of salience are useful, remember that any area in a buffer around a border can now be characterized by a value from 1 to 4, which can be used in data analyses. A four-value scale was created to indicate areas with one important feature up through those with four or more. The size of the circles also helps indicate the level of salience. And, again, a color map of salience is important by demonstrating how borders may differ in their importance—in terms of where people live, where the capital city is located, and where significant elements of the transportation, military, or economic systems are situated. Portions of borders where more of these items are located (within a 50,000-meter buffer of the border) could be seen as more important or salient (the areas in red or orange) than segments without population centers or economic, military, or transportation facilities. As with opportunity for interaction, this representation of the salience of borders permits us to differentiate whole borders, to differentiate portions of long borders, and to make sense as to why some borders might be seen as more important than others—why changes or events across some borders might generate more uncertainty than occurrences across other borders.

The use of a GIS data set, then, gives us a new mechanism for operationalizing a state's borders. A GIS system has been used to create new data. Through the indexes generated, we can attach values to a single dyadic border or border segment. These values will indicate the ease of interaction provided by that border and the importance of any particular border or border segment. These two dimensions can be used separately or combined.

A New Data Set on the "Nature" of Borders

As shown in Table 6.1, the GIS-generated maps can be reduced to a relatively compact data set useful for quantitative analysis. For each of the 301 contiguous land borders between states, ten variables have been developed, which can be transformed into a variety of nominal, ordinal, and interval measures. For any dyad border, or *arc* (see the example of Israel's borders used in Table 6.1), we can present the length of that border in kilometers and the area under the buffers created from that border. From these two variables we can present the percentage of each border that falls into categories 4 through 1 (or, red through dark green in the color figures). This can be done for ease of interaction or saliency. Knowing the length of the arc, the area under the buffer along it, and the percentage of each category permits the analyst to use interval data or broadly based categories such as high salience or low salience. Note also that Table 6.1 provides a weighted average for each border in terms of ease of interaction or salience, showing the average value across the whole border. This data set includes 151 states with land borders, which generate 301 separate contiguous land borders between states. The states in this group thus average almost four borders each.

Table 6.2 provides descriptive data on the total set of borders, using the weighted averages. For example, we see

Table 6.1 Components of a New Data Set: The Example of Israel's Borders

Israel's border with:	Egypt	Jordan	Lebanon	Syria
Length (km)	220	410	110	92
Area (sq km)	21,108	39,282	8,944	10,184
Percent Ease of Interaction Category:				
1	7.41	28.97	29.58	19.06
2	4.44	18.13	24.78	12.43
3	86.03	50.24	42.56	61.55
4	2.12	2.67	3.08	6.96
Percent Salience Category:				
1	91.62	92.34	81.50	90.23
2	6.18	6.31	11.48	7.22
3	2.20	1.35	6.13	2.56
4	0.00	0.00	0.88	0.00
Weighted Average of Ease of Interaction	2.83	2.27	2.19	2.56
Weighted Average of Salience	1.11	1.09	1.26	1.12

Table 6.2 GIS-Based Data Set: Summary Statistics across All Borders (Based on Weighted Averages of Each Border)

	Ease of Interaction	Salience	Length
Minimum	1.195	1.000	3.0
Maximum	3.296	1.369	6900.0
Median	2.800	1.013	520.0
Mean	2.597	1.044	792.8
Standard Deviation	0.500	0.071	863.8

$N = 301$ cases; weighted averages (except for length)

that the average salience is quite low, barely getting above 1.000 (with a maximum value of 1.369 on the 4.000 scale). This means that although we find many "red" areas (scale of 4.000) on the maps, they constitute only very small portions of the total border. The values for ease of interaction are much higher. Interestingly, the border with the highest salience score exists between Moldova and Ukraine. In many ways this should not be surprising, because until 1991 this was only an *internal* border, or the equivalent of the border between Connecticut and Massachusetts. With a weighted average of 1.342, the German-Dutch border is the next highest. A cluster of relatively high salience borders, as well as high ease of interaction borders, are found among the original members of the European Economic Community (EEC) (we will discuss this further in Chapter 8).

How might this approach to geopolitics be of use to international relations scholars? Let us begin with a broad point about geopolitics and the study of international relations. One basic issue raised in Most and Starr (1989), applied to our earlier discussion of alliances, was that researchers needed to be much clearer as to the broader concepts that were really under investigation, so that their models and the resulting research designs could be more logically and fully specified. Perhaps "borders" can be used in some research for reasons that are innate to "borderness"—that they *separate* entities from one another. However, as discussed, most uses of borders involve their representation of proximity—that is, entities are *close* to one another, *important* to one another, and have an *enhanced ability to interact* with one another. But, does the existence of a border actually represent these notions? Borders that are difficult to traverse, either commercially or militarily, may not fit this idea of proximity. Borders that are "buffered" by empty and meaningless spaces may not fit this idea of proximity.

Conversely, legal borders in the contemporary globalized world may be meaningless in terms of full permeability and high levels of transactions—as in the European Union.

A wide array of research questions based on the assumption that borders indicate proximity, salience, and ease of interaction may be addressed by a borders data set that digs into the nature of the border. Is it the *nature* of the border rather than the mere existence of a border or the *numbers* of borders that affect conflictual or cooperative behavior? What about Boulding's "critical boundaries"? What is the relationship between borders and critical boundaries? Are attempts to match the two reflected in interstate conflict or conflict over territory in particular? The GIS data described here can help us see the effects of critical boundaries in the Israeli case.

Although perhaps not an entirely novel interpretation, the visualizations of Israel's borders clearly highlight how Israel's critical boundary was vulnerable, until the 1967 war, from its three neighbors who were also enduring rivals: Egypt, Syria, and Jordan. The map for the ease of interaction of Israel's borders shows that the areas of the greatest ease of interaction are along the coast and along the basically north–south segment of the West Bank bulge that most closely approaches the coast (capturing particularly the road and transportation networks in those areas). The map of the salience measure also indicates the importance of the area between this border segment and the coast. Until 1967 a border with both high ease of interaction and high salience constituted part of Israel's contiguous land border with Jordan.

One consequence of the 1967 war was to remove the vulnerability of this border by moving the legal border outward to one with both low ease of interaction and low salience. That is, the GIS-generated maps show that the border along the Jordan River Valley, created after the 1967 war, is an area with the greatest difficulty for interaction (as is the border on the Golan Heights) and one with few population areas or important facilities. The maps demonstrate a case where the legal boundary and critical boundary did not appear to coincide. Much of Israeli strategic thinking since 1967 was based on fighting a war at or outside the Jordan River border, and *not* along the border of the western bulge of the West Bank area. Indeed, examination of maps presenting the progress of the 1973 Yom Kippur war indicate that even the deepest penetration of Egyptian forces moved only thirty to fifty miles into the Sinai; and the deepest penetration of Syrian forces never reached the pre-1967 border.

Conclusion

In this book we have stressed that one key aspect of borders is that they affect the interaction opportunities of states, constraining or expanding the possibilities of interaction that are available to them. States that share borders will tend to have a greater ease of interaction with one another. Secondly, borders also have an impact on the willingness of decision makers to choose certain policy options, in that they act as indicators of areas of great importance or salience. The ARC/INFO GIS permits us to operationalize and investigate these two dimensions. Using data available in the different data layers found in ARC/INFO's Digital Chart of the World, I constructed indexes both of ease of interaction and of salience. They can be used to characterize any border (or arc) or border segment on the globe. We can now go beyond simply noting the existence of a border or its length. Through the indexes generated, we can attach values to the ease of interaction that a border or any border segment provides and to the importance of any particular border or border segment. The GIS-generated indexes permit us to tap both dimensions and to use them singly or combined, depending on the research question under consideration.

There are, as always, limitations to the data. Perhaps the most important is that the data set is derived only from the 1992 Digital Chart of the World and, therefore, does not constitute a time series. That is, the data reflect a limited temporal domain. This is the "heroic" assumption discussed in note 3. However, because such variables as the hypsography of the terrain or the identity of the national capital are relatively stable and other variables change only slowly (e.g., the building of railroads), our assumption is that the indexes can indeed retain validity as a rough surrogate for the ease of interaction and salience for the time frame mentioned: back in time for twenty to twenty-five years and forward for a decade to a decade and a half. This assumption also holds because the index for salience uses a wide variety of indicators in order to capture the specific circumstances of a range of countries. For this reason, scholars wishing to extend a version of the salience index back in time could similarly identify state capitals, major population centers, and those locations (military installations, ports, railheads) they deem to be of importance to the military, economic, and political infrastructure of states. For ease of interaction, scholars could identify physical features that would impede the movement of people and goods, such as mountains, swamps, or deserts. Historical records could indicate the location of major rail lines or, prior to the development of the railroad, major overland roads/trade routes. These indicators could provide at least a rough approximation of the ease of interaction index.

I have found that this GIS-based approach to borders, even with its limitations, allows us to come at the relationships between international relations and geopolitical factors in useful ways. Here, we used the example of Israel to show how the GIS data may be provided in maps as well as in a data set available for analysis. Matching the maps that were generated against the historical record of Israel's armed conflicts with its neighbors, including the movement of troops and armor, provides strong face validity for the measures of ease of interaction and salience (see especially Starr 2000). In the next chapter, we will provide other examples of how these data could help revisit previous hypotheses regarding geopolitics and conflict as well as new ways to study conflict in the global arena. In Chapter 8, we will indicate how this data set might also be of use in specifically studying the development of cooperation.

CHAPTER 7
THE NATURE OF BORDERS AND CONFLICT

GIS, Concepts, and Measures

In the last chapter, I demonstrated one way in which geographic tools could be applied to geopolitics and the study of international relations. GIS approaches have the potential to make important contributions to IR research. I have tried to show how they have permitted a reconceptualization of borders and to demonstrate the ability of GIS to help generate data previously unavailable. In combination, these two contributions reflect the spirit of Thomas Kuhn (1962)—with the creation of new methods of measurement that lead to a method of "exploration"—where the newly available data can be useful in suggesting additional or original theories or hypotheses.

For example, borders as a measure of distance or proximity have generally been used as a "discrete or categorical, typically binary" (Gleditsch and Ward 2001, 742) measure. This view of distance, as an "on/off" dummy variable, although useful in many studies, is limited because a measure indicating only the presence or absence of a border makes a number of assumptions that cannot be assessed. In my research using the GIS data on the nature of borders, I have worked on the assumption that deeper investigation into the characteristics of borders allows us more closely to specify relationships and revisit analyses of territory and conflict in order to produce more accurate descriptions of their relationships.

A number of these studies will be discussed in this chapter and the next. The results of these analyses support the design and purpose of the GIS project of reconceptualizing borders as it breaks away from the dichotomous characterization of states as contiguous or noncontiguous. Many of the results do not fit the expectations of the "standard" adversarial proximity conflict model and demonstrate that the border reconceptualization presented here can be used to investigate a number of related questions in the study of international politics involving *both* cooperative processes and conflictual ones. It is also important to note that having this data set—one that goes beyond the on/off measure of contiguity—can also show us where simple contiguity *does* indeed work well and where deeper measurements may not be necessary. In fact, the first two sections that follow come to this conclusion. They are then followed by the presentation of studies that revisit IR hypotheses and present more complex results—results that allow us to move on to cooperation as well as conflict.

Revisiting Hypotheses on Conflict: Borders, Alliances, and Diffusion

In my initial analyses of the diffusion of armed conflict, the presence or absence of borders was used as a key explanatory variable. Some studies used just contiguous homeland borders; some also used cross-water or colonial borders. In a variety of these studies, it was clear that a positive spatial diffusion process was involved. But, using the on/off variable asking whether two states were contiguous or not, a number of questions were left unanswered. For example, which *types* of borders are most or least related to spatial diffusion? In my work with Ben Most on the diffusion of conflict (e.g., Most and Starr 1980), we investigated whether states that were subjected to the "treatment" of having a warring border nation (WBN) were more likely to become involved in conflict than those without such a treatment. In my work with Randolph Siverson (e.g., 1991), we added the effect of having a warring alliance partner (WAP).

One finding that could be investigated with the GIS data was presented in Siverson and Starr (1991). There we noted that the relationship between joining an ongoing war and being subjected to WBNs or WAPs is one of "loose necessity." That is, many states have treatments as indicated by a WBN or WAP but do not join wars. In fact, having only *one* treatment (only one WBN or WAP) appeared to have almost no effect on the behavior of states. Thus, the GIS data set permits the investigation of the *nature of the borders* that separate the state from its WBN or WAP. Is it simply "borderness" in some general sense (measured by presence or absence of a border) or the more specific qualities measured in the GIS data that are involved? Looking only at borders (not alliances), a first cut at whether greater ease of interaction or greater salience are associated with the diffusion of either interstate or intrastate conflict provides no support for hypotheses that diffusion would be more likely to occur with borders that had greater ease of interaction or greater salience. For *interstate* conflict, we see that within the limited time period surveyed (across thirty to thirty-five years), violent conflict in the international system tended *not* to diffuse or grow. The small number of cases that were available for analysis was itself a striking finding. For the larger number of internationalized *intrastate* conflicts, the nature of the border appeared not to have an effect on the diffusion of conflict. We could not have made this comparison using only the original data set developed by Starr and Most.

Revisiting Borders as Part of the War Puzzle (a First Cut)

As discussed in Chapter 3, a large part of the considerable research devoted to borders and territory suggests that territorial contiguity is a major determinant of whether a state will go to war with another state. Indeed, as a significant piece of "the war puzzle," Vasquez (1993) suggests that territorial contiguity is the source of conflict most likely to result in war. However, perhaps simple contiguity may not be the critical factor. Dropping one level of analysis lower, Vasquez also hypothesized that topographical features of the border between two states also affect the probability that states will go to war. Specifically, he hypothesized that borders that coincide with natural frontiers or that traverse uninhabited regions or are seen as having little value are much less likely to provoke wars than dissimilar borders and border areas (note that his hypotheses are about both opportunity and willingness).

The data set generated by the GIS project provides an ideal way to test Vasquez's hypotheses about dropping one level of analysis lower. Three different groups of conflict dyads were selected for this analysis: a set of twenty-two enduring rivalry dyads (Goertz and Diehl 1993, 1995); a set of twenty-seven territorial dispute dyads (Huth 1996); and a set of sixty-one militarized interstate dispute dyads (using 1996 militarized interstate dispute [MID] data). These cases were selected for pairs of states that shared a contiguous land border and where the conflict (or series of conflicts) involved fell into the broad temporal band covered by the GIS data. In order to test the null hypothesis that borders coinciding with natural frontiers (a greater difficulty in my measure of ease of interaction) have either no effect on the probability of armed conflict, or make armed conflict more likely, one must compare the nature of borders where conflict has occurred with those where conflict has not occurred. The same is true for the effect of the perceived importance (the GIS measure of salience) of a border area.

One strategy would be to compare the nature of conflict borders with all other borders in the system. However, this strategy is flawed because it fails to account for differences in government and for differences in the propensity of individual states to enter into wars. Instead, a more conservative strategy is employed that can take these differences into account: testing for statistically significant differences between conflict dyad borders (the shared contiguous homeland border between two states) and the remaining borders of the two states that form the conflict dyad. An alternative hypothesis is also examined. This hypothesis posits that rather than the nature of the border being important, the length of the border is the primary distinguishing factor between conflict borders and non-conflict borders. The longer a border is, the greater the opportunity for interaction and, therefore, conflict.

The weighted averages for ease of interaction and salience for enduring rivalry borders were compared with the remaining borders of states in the enduring rivalry. Of the eighteen comparisons made (nine each for ease of interaction and salience), surprisingly, not a single category measuring the nature of the border shows a statistically significant ($p=0.10$) difference in means. On this basis, one can conclude that the nature of the borders of a state engaged in an enduring rivalry does not significantly improve our chances of predicting which neighboring state will be the enduring rival. On the other hand, the alternative null hypothesis that no statistical difference exists between the *mean border length* for enduring rivalry conflict dyads and the mean length of remaining enduring rival borders can be rejected. This suggests that based solely on the knowledge of the *length of the borders* of a state engaged in an enduring rivalry, we can better predict which state will be the enduring rivalry conflict dyad partner. Conflict dyads taken from Huth's (1996) territorial disputes data set show similar results.

The final set of analyses uses the MID data. Similar tests regarding the differences between the means of conflict dyads and the remaining borders of conflict parties were conducted. The MID data are much more inclusive than those of either Goertz and Diehl or Huth and generate more useable dyads for analysis.[1] Nevertheless, a phenomenon similar to that found in the Huth territorial dispute data exists in the MID data. Once again the analysis supports the null hypotheses—that borders that are more difficult to cross and borders that are less salient/important do not lower the likelihood that states will go to war with that neighbor. However, differences in the mean length of borders for conflict dyads and non-conflict borders for conflict parties remain statistically significant.

These initial analyses do not support Vasquez's notion that dropping to lower levels of interaction opportunity increases the ability to explain war (which I had assumed in creating the GIS data set). The alternative hypothesis, that the nature of the border doesn't matter but that what does matter is the length of the border, does receive broad support from an analysis of three major conflict data sets. Still, the finding that the length of the border matters does suggest that our general concern with interaction opportunities *was generally correct* in terms of territorial contiguity. It also suggests that, indeed, Wesley (1962) was on the right track. It also supports other analyses by Vasquez (1993), in which he demonstrates the importance that *any* territory has to states. Territory appears to be important. The opportunities for territory to become part of an armed conflict are increased by the length of contiguous territory and not by more specific GIS-generated measures of opportunity and willingness.

However, these analyses *do* provide an indication of the utility of the GIS-based conceptualization and data set. The results of these analyses demonstrate that such a data set can be used to investigate a number of related questions, for example: What sorts of borders can be found between states in enduring rivalries? What is the nature of the territory over which conflicts arise? Goertz and Diehl (1992), Holsti (1991), and Huth (1996), for example, focus on territory per se as a *cause* of war—as both the issue over which war breaks out and as a factor that increases the stakes of a war. Such analyses provide us with a very important alternative hypothesis: it is territory—any territory—that creates an opportunity for conflict that serves as the issue for war and that makes the stakes worth fighting over. What the GIS-based data set has done is to permit analysts to test these competing hypotheses.

Revisiting International Relations Hypotheses: Crisis Analysis

In a set of studies with Dale Thomas (see Starr and Thomas 2002), we investigated the relationships between the ease of interaction and salience measures and the analysis of crisis, revisiting hypotheses investigated in Michael Brecher and Jonathan Wilkenfeld (1997). Here, our analyses did indeed indicate that the nature of the border *does* matter in regard to the choice of a crisis management technique, whether the crisis was part of an ongoing protracted conflict (ease of interaction), and how it was resolved (salience).

Brecher and Wilkenfeld's *A Study of Crisis* (1997) is perhaps the most comprehensive study of post–World War I crises, both in the scope of the crises studied and in the questions asked regarding crisis. The authors provide synopses of 412 different crises and attempt to break new ground by analyzing specific hypotheses relating to polarity, geography, ethnicity, democracy, protracted conflict, violence, and third-party intervention. *A Study of Crisis* incorporates two different levels of crisis: a foreign policy level and an international level. According to the authors, a foreign policy crisis exists when top-level decision makers perceive (1) a threat to one or more basic values, (2) a limited time for response, and (3) a heightened likelihood of military hostilities. Alternatively, an international crisis is defined by two conditions: "(1) a change in type and/or an increase in intensity of disruptive, that is, hostile verbal or physical interactions between two or more states" with a corresponding increase in the likelihood of military hostilities that "(2) destabilizes their relationship and challenges the structure of an international system—global, dominant, or subsystem" (Brecher and Wilkenfeld 1997, 4–5).

As with war/militarized conflict more generally, Brecher and Wilkenfeld's analysis of geographical factors incorporates adversarial proximity as a leading determinant of crisis behavior. The authors specifically test four hypotheses related to crisis behavior:

- the greater the proximity of the crisis adversaries, the more likely it is that the crisis will be triggered by violence
- the greater the proximity of the crisis adversaries, the more likely it is that violence will be employed in crisis management
- the greater the proximity of the crisis adversaries, the more likely it is that the crisis will terminate in agreement
- the greater the proximity of the crisis adversaries, the more likely it is that the crisis will be part of a protracted conflict.

Following much of the work on proximity/borders and conflict, Brecher and Wilkenfeld (1997) contend that proximity provides greater opportunities for military action as a crisis trigger and as a crisis management technique. Similarly, because of the increased opportunities for interaction, crisis incidents between countries that are closer to one another are more likely to be part of an ongoing protracted conflict than those between distant countries. The authors also argue greater proximity necessitates less ambiguous outcomes than can be tolerated by distant opponents. However, even if the Brecher and Wilkenfeld logic holds, it may only hold to a point or under a specific set of conditions, because proximity *may* also be related to increased interdependence and integration.

Although cooperation within the European Union context will be addressed in the next chapter, our approach to the study of crisis using the GIS data led naturally to considerations of what ease of interaction and salience might mean for cooperation among states. That is, highly permeable and salient borders may produce qualitatively distinct behavior. For example, the ease of interaction and salience of border areas in northwestern Europe have—based on Karl Deutsch's (e.g., Deutch et al. 1957) social communication model of integration—most likely contributed to the area's moving from high levels of conflict to high levels of cooperation. Relations between states with highly permeable and salient borders have shown a tendency toward interdependence/integration, making military conflict less likely and agreement more likely. We argued that this phenomenon derives from the central place of transactions in Deutsch's model of integration—by acting as an indicator of mutual relevance. Deutsch argued that high and continuous transaction flows were one precondition for integration (security communities), with transactions a key part of the integration process.

Given the role of transactions in Deutschian models of integration and their potential as indicators of growing interdependence and integration, then greater ease of interaction along a border also generates opportunities for positive interaction as well as opportunities for conflict. It is the latter relationship that was central to the interaction opportunity model as it was first developed, measured simply by the presence or absence of a border. The GIS index for ease of interaction permits a more complete investigation of the effects of borders with different levels of ease and salience.

Reanalyzing Crises with the GIS Data Set

If the nature of borders is important, and the opportunity for increased positive interactions also exists, then relying on Brecher and Wilkenfeld's categories of *contiguous, near-neighbor,* and *distant* to operationalize adversarial proximity obscures the possible effects of an interdependence/integration process.

And, of course, if such a linkage exists, it will weaken findings favoring what I have called adversarial proximity hypotheses: simply, the closer you are the more conflict you will have (e.g., Brecher and Wilkenfeld 1997; Starr and Most 1976; Vasquez 1993). Different types of contiguous borders may lead to different types of behavior. Consequently, we need to disentangle these possible behaviors, and reconceptualizing borders using GIS allows exactly this. In the crisis analyses we also combined the indexes for ease of interaction and salience into a single measure—which we called Vital Borders. The higher the category for "vitalness," the greater the ease of interaction and the greater the salience or importance of the border.

Recall that "heroic" assumption of the GIS data that they can be usefully applied backward from 1992 for a period of approximately twenty to twenty-five years and forward for at least a decade. In reanalyzing the Brecher and Wilkenfeld (1997) data, the cutoff point is set so that all crises ended in 1980 or later.[2] The Brecher and Wilkenfeld hypotheses were tested using the traditional measures of proximity and represent a "baseline" for the analyses using the reconceptualized borders. The null hypotheses are that no differences exist between the contiguous and near-neighbor/distant groups on crisis trigger, management technique, and outcome, and whether the crisis is part of an ongoing protracted conflict. The statistical tests indicate there is a difference in the crisis trigger behavior for contiguous and for near-neighbor/distant parties to crises. External violence is much more likely for contiguous parties (58 percent of the cases) than near-neighbor/distant parties (42 percent). However, nonviolent triggers, internal challenges, and nonviolent military triggers are much more likely for near-neighbor/distant parties (76 percent of the cases) than for contiguous parties (24 percent). Contiguous border crises are much more likely to end in agreement (56 percent of the cases) than near-neighbor/distant crises (18 percent). On the other hand, near-neighbor/distant crises are much more likely instead to have a unilaterally imposed resolution, a tacit resolution, or other ending (82 percent). This is a statistically significant difference, as is the behavior of the two categories on whether the crisis was part of a protracted conflict. Also important is that, contrary to the Brecher and Wilkenfeld hypotheses, 76 percent of near-neighbor/distant crises as opposed to only 46 percent of contiguous crises were part of an ongoing protracted conflict. Interestingly, this appears to be the result of an interdependence/integration dynamic suppressing the expected conflict dynamic.

Breaking contiguous borders down into those with high ease of interaction and border salience and those with low ease of interaction and border salience should allow us to disentangle these two dynamics. The GIS border data set's weighted measures of ease of interaction, salience, and "vitalness" offer three alternative methods of reconceptualizing contiguous borders. These can be supplemented by the previously mentioned fourth method of using border length. If an interdependence/integration effect exists, we expect that it will be strongest for those countries with vital borders, that is, those with the highest ease of interaction, border salience, and combination of the two. To the extent that length captures opportunities for interaction, we would also expect that the effect will be strongest for those countries with the longest borders.[3]

Interestingly, *each of the border measures except for border length lends support to the interdependence/integration argument.* Each of the Brecher and Wilkenfeld hypotheses was retested using the four different characterizations of borders. The Brecher-Wilkenfeld hypotheses reflect the adversarial proximity view,

which typically measures the ability to interact and the importance for involved states, through the categories of contiguous,
near-neighbor, and distant. This logic could then be applied
to our GIS measures, such that the more vital (permeable
and salient) a border is, the more likely military conflict will
be part of crisis behavior. However, we can now take the
group of contiguous states and separate them into high and
low vitalness; we can do the same for the near-neighbor/
distant group. Thus, using the GIS measures we were able to
weigh the relative merits of the interdependence/integration
argument and the adversarial proximity conflict approach.

When contiguity is broken down this way, the effects on
crisis management and whether the crisis is part of a protracted
conflict support the interdependence/integration argument.
That is, when countries in crisis are contiguous—which should
be related to more crisis and conflict and less effective conflict
management—and are *also* in the group of borders with the
greatest ease of interaction, the *relationships are reversed*. What we
have called the interdependence/integration dynamic appears
to suppress the conflict dynamic hypothesized in previous literature—for the lower three quartiles the expected relationship
holds, but this is reversed for the highest quartile. The second
measurement of the nature of borders is salience. Reexamin-
ing the same relationships using border salience produces less
clear-cut results, but also tends to support the interdependence/
integration effect. The third measurement of the nature of
borders is vitalness. Re-operationalizing contiguity from
on/off to quartiles of the weighted average for vitalness (the
combination of ease of interaction and salience) also produces
support for an interdependence/integration dynamic. Crises
occurring across borders that fall into the upper quartile of
the weighted vitalness measure are more likely to be managed

through nonmilitary or nonviolent military means than those in the lower three quartiles. Furthermore, countries sharing vital borders are much less likely to be involved in a protracted conflict crisis (17 percent of the cases) than those in the lower quartiles (67 percent). The last measure of the nature of borders uses length. As noted, the length of borders *does not* appear to make a statistically significant difference for crisis triggers, management techniques, and outcomes, or for whether crises are part of ongoing protracted conflicts.

This reanalysis of the Brecher and Wilkenfeld International Crisis Behavior (ICB) data with the alternative GIS conceptualizations of contiguity suggests that findings based on a distant, near-neighbor, and contiguous categorization of cases are masking important dynamics that need to be explored. A dynamic that reflects the Deutschian model of integration—with its attendant focus on transactions—definitely appears to be affecting countries with borders at the *upper ends* of the measurement scales for ease of interaction, salience, and vitalness. This is an important finding, not only because an interdependence/integration dynamic exists, but also because the presence of this dynamic statistically suppresses the conflict dynamic *normally found* in hypotheses relating to contiguity.

It is important to remember that the cases involved in analyzing the ICB crises using the GIS data set *all* have contiguous borders, which have been shown across many studies to increase the probability of conflict. Given this existence of contiguity, what factors are associated with a greater probability of violent or cooperative behaviors in regard to crises? The analyses here indicate that *high levels* of ease of interaction, salience, and vitalness (and not length of border) affect nonviolent and more cooperative behaviors. Factors that would facilitate more frequent transactions and more meaningful transactions (as possibly represented by salience) are related to the development of webs of interdependence and possibly nascent elements of integration, as would be argued in Deutschian models. In other words, two different populations of contiguous borders may exist: those with a *conflict dynamic* (which exhibit a lower ease of interaction/salience/vitalness, but perhaps greater length) and those with a *cooperation/integration dynamic* (which exhibit a higher ease of interaction/salience/vitalness).

Revisiting Borders, Territory, and Conflict (a Second Cut)

The study just presented uncovered the possibility that contiguous borders might be of two general types with different effects on conflict and cooperation. This would not have been possible without the GIS data set. Following up on these analyses, a second study by Starr and Thomas (e.g., 2005) continued the investigation of contiguity and conflict and again focused on the two contrasting views relating contiguity and conflict. The first is the "standard" adversarial proximity view that the easier a border is to cross and the more salient the border, the *higher* the probability of militarized dispute. The second view, deriving from Deutschian integration theory (based on high levels of transactions), proposed that the easier a border is to cross and the more salient the border, the *lower* the probability of militarized dispute. Each view, however, represents a linear (positive or negative) relationship between the nature of borders and conflict. As developed in what follows, Starr and Thomas (2005) proposed a curvilinear relationship, with the low occurrence of conflict at both the lowest *and* highest levels of ease of interaction (opportunity) and salience (willingness). That is, we proposed—and found—that conflict is most likely where the expected utility of conflict is greatest—in the middle—where states have both the opportunity and willingness to engage in conflict.

Back to Vasquez and Deutsch

We have discussed the "standard" view and identified several (of the many) scholars who have used this view as the basis for analysis. For simplicity, we can refer to this as the Vasquez model—as it was very important to the development of Vasquez's "war puzzle." He argued that greater proximity and greater value of territory would raise the probability of conflict and that borders that were difficult to cross and were of little value would lower the probability of conflict.

Yet we have also presented models that suggest just the opposite is true. In Karl Deutsch's social communication model of integration, transaction flows were seen as central to the process by which integration took place and security communities were formed. According to Deutsch, countries are "clusters of population, united by grids of communication flows and transport systems, and separated by thinly settled or nearly empty territories" (cited in Dougherty and Pfaltzgraff 1990, 435). The Deutschian study of how countries become integrated focuses on these transaction grids (see Deutsch et al. 1957 and 1967). Continuous communication and transaction linkages are presented by Deutsch as one of nine conditions for the creation of security communities. Because security communities are at the heart of Deutsch's view of integration, we should describe them more fully:

> A security community is a group of people which has
> become "integrated." By integration we mean the attain-
> ment, within a territory, and of institutions and practices
> strong enough and widespread enough to assure ... de-
> pendable expectations of "peaceful change" among its
> population. By sense of community we mean a belief ...
> that common social problems must and can be resolved
> by processes of peaceful change. (Deutsch et al. 1957, 5)

This Deutschian definition of integration focuses on peace
and the conditions for peace; but it does more. A security
community involves not only the absence of war ("negative
peace"), but more importantly, the absence of even consideration of the military option in the interactions of the states
within the security community.

Roger Cobb and Charles Elder (1970, 8) go straight to the
essential Deutschian relationship between transactions and integration: "The third basic notion from communications theory is
the idea that 'transactions flow ... establish[es] mutual relevance
of actors. An actor with whom you have very much to do is
relevant to you ...' Given this assumption, the level of interaction,
or transaction, between the members of two social units may be
taken as a behavioral measure of their mutual relevance." They
further observe, "Deutsch ... finds that all successful security
communities have a multiplicity of transaction channels per-
forming a variety of common functions and purposes. Indeed,
a high rate of transactional exchange within an area may mean
that the community achieves a degree of integration" (1970, 24).
The results of Cobb and Elder's empirical study link the exchange
of transactions to mutual relevance and then mutual relevance
to greater levels of interstate collaboration. For Bruce Russett,
the mutual relevance of integration leading to a security community is represented by "responsiveness"—or, "the probability

that requests emanating from one state to the other will be met favorably" (1974, 329). In looking at integration defined as either responsiveness or security communities, Russett (1974) finds that transactions describe integration, predict integration, make integration possible, and even cause integration.

Given the role of transactions in Deutschian models of integration and their potential as indicators of growing inter-dependence and integration, then greater ease of interaction along a border also generates opportunities for positive inter-action as well as opportunities for conflict. Highly permeable borders might also indicate the existence of active free markets. A number of analysts have linked free trade with cooperative/peaceful interactions (e.g., Russett and Oneal 2001, investigating relationships among the elements of the Kantian triad and peace). Note that these views of transactions are also consistent with the interaction opportunity model.

Thus, we have two sets of specific testable hypotheses regarding the impact of the "nature" of borders on conflict. These hypotheses can be phrased as

- the easier a border is to cross, the greater the likelihood that the border will be a conflict or dispute border (Vasquez)
- the more salient a border is, the greater the likelihood that the border will be a conflict or dispute border (Vasquez)
- the easier a border is to cross, the less likelihood that the border will be a conflict or dispute border (Deutsch)
- the more salient a border is, the less likelihood that the border will be a conflict or dispute border (Deutsch).

Although both sets of hypotheses push scholars to move beyond the simple on/off indicator of contiguity, they postulate mutually exclusive monotonic relationships.

Figure 7.1   Contradictory Hypotheses on the Nature of Borders and the Likelihood of Conflict

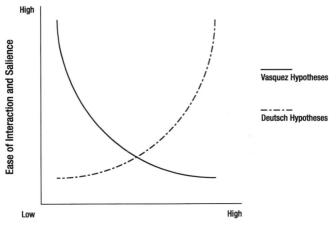

Importantly, notions of cost curves and utility underlie all four of the above hypotheses. These are shown in Figure 7.1. As the ease of interaction increases (opportunity), the costs of projecting a state's power across a border decrease and thus decrease the costs of violent conflict. Similarly, based on the logic found in Vasquez, the value of highly salient border areas makes an actor's marginal cost of escalating conflict to violence or war (related to willingness) much lower when such territory is threatened, whereas, on the other hand, low border salience increases an actor's marginal costs of violent conflict. Yet, based on the Deutschian perspective, ease of interaction and border salience are likely to coincide with the development of integration effects. As states become increasingly integrated, the costs of violent conflict—a militarized interstate dispute—between them increase as well.

Figure 7.2   Linear vs. U-Shaped Hypotheses
on the Probability of Conflict*

	Border Ease of Interaction, Salience, and "Vitalness"		
	Low	Medium	High
Vasquez	CONFLICT	CONFLICT	CONFLICT
Deutsch	CONFLICT	CONFLICT	CONFLICT
Starr and Thomas	CONFLICT	CONFLICT	CONFLICT

* The increased likelihood of conflict is visually depicted by an increased font size

Interestingly and importantly, the *intersection of the two cost curves represents the region with the lowest cost* for a militarized interstate dispute—and thus the highest probability for armed conflict. On this basis, we can propose that both the Vasquez and Deutschian hypotheses are *independently incomplete*. However, the insights of the two can be combined in a potentially powerful explanatory model. Rather than the relationship between the "nature" of borders and conflict being monotonically increasing or decreasing, we propose that the relationship is concave: the *lowest* levels of opportunity and border region salience should correspond to proportionally low incidences of conflict as should the *highest* levels of opportunity and border region salience, whereas the middle range of opportunity and salience should have proportionally the highest incidences of conflict. Thus, rather than testing just the Vasquez or Deutsch views, we investigated three rival hypotheses, which are presented in Figure 7.2.

Competing Hypotheses: Enduring Rivalries and MIDs

The GIS data set allowed us to evaluate empirically the theoretical claims of the two seemingly distinct bodies of literature and hypotheses, as well as our synthesis. Which finds the greatest support? In order to give both the Vasquez and Deutsch hypotheses an equal opportunity and to allow for the possibility that both may be partially true, the border measures were divided into three categories: borders falling in the lowest 20 percent of weighted measures for ease of interaction, salience, and "vitalness"; borders falling in the middle 60 percent of weighted measures for ease of interaction, salience, and "vitalness"; and borders falling in the highest 20 percent of weighted measures for ease of interaction, salience, and "vitalness."

As seen in Figure 7.2, if the Vasquez hypotheses hold, then one would expect to see the lowest levels of conflict for the lowest 20 percent of cases and the highest levels of conflict for the highest 20 percent of cases. If the Deutschian integration/ interdependence hypotheses hold, then one would expect to see the highest levels of conflict for the lowest 20 percent of cases and the lowest levels of conflict for the highest 20 percent of cases. Finally, if both hypotheses sets have partial merit, then one would likely see low levels of conflict for both the upper and lower 20 percent but relatively high levels for the middle 60 percent, as in the Starr and Thomas synthesis.

Analyses were performed on two conflict data sets for cases falling within the GIS data time frame: enduring rivalries and MIDs. Looking at the nature of enduring rivalry borders, neither the Vasquez nor Deutschian hypotheses completely hold. Rather, the concave relationship hypothesized in Figure 7.2 is found: The combination of constrained opportunity through limited ease of interaction and low salience does reduce the probability of a border becoming an enduring rivalry border, but so does the combination of easy interaction and high border salience. The highest probability of a border becoming an enduring rivalry border lies in the middle region, where the *apparent costs of conflict are lowest.* The same is true when examining the borders between states that had MIDs.[4]

These results suggest a number of important points. First, governments appear less likely to act/react in a conflictual manner (and a *militarized* manner) over low-salience border areas. These include borders that exhibit relatively low population concentrations and, compared with the length of the border, a dearth of infrastructure. Strong arguments have been presented by Vasquez (1993), by Goertz and Diehl (1992), and by Huth (1996), among others, that it is territory per se that generates conflict and war, both as the issue over which war breaks out and as a factor that increases the stakes of a war. We actually found the same when looking at the nature of borders and the diffusion or spread of conflict, as described before. Such arguments are based on the proposition that it is territory—any territory—that creates an opportunity for conflict, serves as the issue for war, and makes the stakes worth fighting over.

It is important to note that such arguments *are not supported* by the inverted U-shaped findings presented here, either for rivalry borders or MID borders. This is especially reflected by the extremely small levels of conflict found for the lowest 20 percent of borders in regard to salience. Second, and also interesting, in these analyses border length fails as a competing explanation for why governments do not act/react conflictually over low-salience border areas: of the thirteen MID borders in the lowest 20 percent of salient borders, seven have above average length and six have below average length. Third, high border salience makes dispute escalation to military conflict unlikely. Governments rely on other means of resolving disputes with countries with which they share neighboring vital border areas. Both of these conditions dampen the probability for escalation to military conflict.

In regard to ease of interaction, we find evidence that governments are less likely to turn to military action in the face of physical constraints on mobility. Low ease of interaction reduces the probability of a border becoming an MID border. Additionally, the surprisingly low probability of a high ease of interaction becoming an MID border suggests that as cross-border interaction becomes easier, transaction flows are also likely to increase, thereby contributing to the creation of a security community. Although other explanations may exist, states appear much less likely to escalate a dispute to military action with neighboring states sharing porous borders.

Conclusion

Once again, borders matter. Whether states share borders has been a principal means of operationalizing proximity. However, simply noting the existence of a shared contiguous land border may not adequately reflect the expected underlying behavior. Although two different views from the literature on the relationship between contiguity and conflict were presented, an alternative curvilinear relationship was proposed, with the low occurrence of conflict at both the lowest and highest levels of ease of interaction and salience. Conflict is most likely where the expected utility of conflict is greatest—in the middle—where states have both the opportunity and willingness to engage in conflict.

The research findings in this chapter have demonstrated the utility of moving beyond a simple on/off dichotomous view of contiguous land borders to examine the terrain and human activity along shared border areas. They have also demonstrated that for some phenomena the relationship between borders/contiguity and conflict behavior is nonlinear. *Neither contribution could have been made* using previously collected data on contiguity. They were only possible with the type of data provided by the GIS project on the nature of borders. A border is not a border is not a border. Territory, per se, is neither a necessary nor sufficient reason for conflict, nor does it automatically create greater opportunity for conflict. Some types of borders are dramatically less likely to lead to military conflict than others, and some types are more likely to lead to cooperative activity.

Scholars of international relations need to account for these differences and incorporate them into their research designs. Additionally, such analyses need to take place within a broader research context in which space and spatiality play a larger role, one coequal with that of time. Ease of interaction and salience represent not only opportunity and willingness but also variation across both time-space and cost-space. The various findings presented in this chapter highlight the importance of incorporating spatial components into the theory and methodology of our research design.

CHAPTER **8**
THE NATURE OF BORDERS AND COOPERATION
INTEGRATION IN THE EUROPEAN UNION

Using GIS Measures to Study Cooperation

A major component of the standard approach to borders and territory suggests that territorial contiguity—whether it provides interaction opportunity or the stakes of conflict, or both—is a major determinant of whether states enter conflicts and whether those conflicts escalate to war. However, as we concluded in the overview of my studies on borders and conflict and in the research discussed in Chapter 7, perhaps simple contiguity may not be the critical factor. Relations between states with highly permeable and salient borders have also shown a tendency toward interdependence/integration and may be more peaceful in terms of greater cooperation and community, or simply have less conflict. Either way, such borders would make military conflict *less* likely and agreement more likely.

Although initially developed to study conflict, the GIS-generated data set on the nature of borders, as we have seen, can also be used to study cooperation. Using the GIS data on the nature of borders, we can say that the ease of interaction and salience of border areas in northwestern Europe have—based on Karl Deutsch's social communication model of integration—most likely contributed to the area moving from high levels of conflict to high levels of cooperation. We have argued that this phenomenon derives from the central place of transactions in Deutsch's model of integration—by acting as an indicator of mutual relevance. Deutsch saw high and continuous transaction flows to be one precondition for integration (security communities), with transactions a key part of the integration process. Here, the nature of borders is used to serve as a proxy for the key role of transaction flows. This chapter provides an initial study that attempts to use the GIS border data to investigate the relationship between conditions of integration and borders. Using the waves of expansion in the European Union, hypotheses deriving from Deutschian theory on the nature of borders are addressed and supported.

Borders and Interdependence/ Integration: A Deutschian View

Using the Most and Starr notion of "stylized facts" (1989, 136), we can begin by simply looking at dyads within the summary of the data produced by the GIS analysis, as presented a couple of chapters back in Table 6.2 (see also Table 8.2). The average salience score across all 301 borders is 1.044, with the highest score being 1.369. As noted, the border with this highest salience score (in 1992) was shared by Moldova and Ukraine, which after seven decades as part of the Soviet Union, essentially shared an internal border. However, recall that the second highest score on salience (1.342) was found for the German-Dutch border, which was never an internal border—but between two countries sharing EEC/EU membership. Similarly, a number of shared borders among the original six members of the EEC exhibit high salience scores. These include Belgium-Netherlands (1.279), Belgium-Germany (1.235), France-Luxembourg (1.227), and France-Germany (1.282). This last border best illustrates the point we're trying to make here.

In addition, because of a high density of road and rail facilities, EU dyads also have the highest weighted averages in terms of ease of interaction. Matched against a world average of 2.597 for ease of interaction, the border with the highest weighted average of ease of interaction is between Belgium and France (3.296). The next three highest are: Belgium-Netherlands (3.291), Germany-Netherlands (3.287), and France-Luxembourg (3.284). That is, the borders of the original core countries of the EU also have borders that look like the *internal* jurisdictional boundaries of states, in terms of both salience and ease of interaction. These results reflect Deutsch's social communication model of integration. We may propose that the high values on ease of interaction and salience of border areas in this region of Europe, one of historically high conflict prior to World War II, both reflect high levels of interaction and, in turn, have helped to increase those levels. In so doing, the ease of interaction across salient borders has most likely contributed to the region moving from high levels of conflict to high levels of cooperation. Relations between states with highly permeable and salient borders have shown a tendency toward interdependence/integration, making military conflict less likely and agreement more likely. As discussed in Chapter 7, for Deutsch, transaction flows were central to the process by which integration took place and security communities were formed. The stylized facts presenting GIS-generated data scores on selected borders illustrate that *certain types* of contiguous borders are related to high levels of transactions, interdependence, and integration.

This Deutschian integration perspective can be used to provide alternative contexts (or interpretations) to the role of borders in separating peoples and the effects those borders might have. The results reported in Chapter 7 based on the Starr and Thomas studies are thus extremely important. They represent a crucial (if understudied) perspective, not only because an interdependence/integration dynamic exists, but also because the presence of this dynamic statistically *suppresses* the conflict dynamic *normally found* in hypotheses relating to contiguity. The GIS project has thus highlighted a new effect: *given* contiguity and the conflict-promoting effects of contiguous borders, as ease of interaction and salience become greater, the more positive effects hypothesized in Deutschian social communication/transaction-based integration theory can be seen.

There exists a natural laboratory for a historical experiment involving the nature of contiguous borders and *cooperative* behavior. We can find such a laboratory in the history of integration that began in Western Europe—moving from the European Coal and Steel Community or ECSC (with a 1951 treaty entering into force in 1952), through the European Economic Community (EEC or Common Market), to the European Union (EU) of today. The broadest question would be this: Is there a relationship between the nature of borders and positive economic and social transaction flows among states? Do borders with greater ease of interaction and greater density of cities and salient (valuable and important) facilities promote and/or reflect the existence of interdependence and integration? The Deutschian model would propose a direct relationship: increases in levels of transactions would lead to greater levels of transactions. It would also propose an indirect relationship: increases in levels of transactions would lead to the development of integration, which in turn would lead to greater levels of transactions. Most of these dynamics can be found in the history of the Schengen Agreements, first established in 1985 by five of the original six members of the ECSC and EEC (without Italy) and officially incorporated into the EU in 1999. Designed as a mechanism to create an area without internal borders, and including countries outside of the EU (and with the UK and Ireland essentially as nonparticipants), it represents both the "borderless world discourse" and the Deutschian transaction feedback loop.

The ease of interaction variable, I propose, can be used as a "surrogate" for the levels of transactions that Deutsch argued would generate and reflect the development of integration. For our initial approach to these questions, we can flip the Deutsch hypothesis around and ask, Does the history of the EU membership (during which integration has both deepened and widened) generate borders with high ease of interaction and salience? Specifically, the following three hypotheses will be investigated:

1. The contiguous land borders that EU members have among themselves will have significantly higher average values for ease of interaction (and salience) than the average values for total world contiguous borders.
2. EU members with the longest history in the EU will share contiguous land borders with other EU members that have the highest average values for ease of interaction (and salience).

3. As new waves of members enter the organization, the contiguous borders they share with other EU members will have lower average values for ease of interaction (and salience).

Design and Analyses: A Necessary Caution

I have already noted one major limitation of the GIS data, which must be highlighted here. The data for this project are from the Digital Chart of the World (DCW), produced by ESRI for the Defense Mapping Agency in 1992. Recall that the data contained in the DCW were derived primarily from maps in the Defense Mapping Agency Operational Navigation Chart series that were used to generate a database covering the entire surface of the earth, with the assumption that the border data generated by the 1992 DCW can be usefully applied backward for approximately twenty to twenty-five years and forward for about another decade. Although I have assumed that the data retain validity as a rough surrogate for the ease of interaction and salience of areas for this time frame, the data *do not permit* the investigation in changes of ease of interaction or salience across time and limit analyses to this approximate time frame. Thus, the border data set does not have multiple data points across time, but is assumed to capture dyadic relations over a thirty- to forty-year time period.

That said, EU membership *does change* across time as seen in Table 8.1. The previous hypotheses are based on the argument that changing membership can begin to capture the complex reciprocal effects of transactions, interdependence, and integration embedded in the social communication model. These relationships are found in Russett's (1974) observation that transactions can describe, predict, and make integration possible—as well as be a causal factor. The GIS data set does permit hypotheses that compare EU borders to the world baselines. It also permits comparisons across the groups of states involved in successive "waves" of expansion. The latter comparisons do allow us to look at *implications* of a Deutschian integration model that includes the complex reciprocal effects of transactions, interdependence, and integration (e.g., see Lave and March 1975), and permit an indirect evaluation of the relationship between the nature of borders and positive relationships. Other forms of transactions, which do permit time-series analyses, will be discussed briefly in the conclusion.

Table 8.1 presents an outline of the growth of the EU from the original six members in 1952 (with the European Coal and Steel Community) through the 2007 expansion, which added Bulgaria and Romania. All told, fifteen countries joined the EU after 1989 and the symbolic end of the Cold War, bringing total

Table 8.1   EU Expansion: "Widening" of EU Membership

1952 [9]*	1973 [2]	1981 [0]	1986 [2]	1995 [3]	2004 [15]	2007 [3]
Belgium	Denmark	Greece	Portugal	Austria	Cyprus	Bulgaria
Italy	Ireland		Spain	Finland	Latvia	Romania
France	United			Sweden	Slovakia	
Luxembourg	Kingdom				Czech Rep.	
Germany	(UK)				Lithuania	
Netherlands					Slovenia	
					Estonia	
					Malta	
					Hungary	
					Poland	

Total states: 27
Total within EU borders: 34

* Number of contiguous land borders created with other EU members by entering states

membership to twenty-seven. These twenty-seven countries generate thirty-four contiguous borders among the EU membership. The data in Table 8.2 provide support for Hypothesis 1, that EU members will have higher average values for ease of interaction and salience than the baseline of total world borders. For both measures, simple t-tests show that their values are statistically significantly higher for the twenty-seven EU states compared with the world figure, and then even higher when comparing the original six EU members to the world. In addition, we can see that ease of interaction and salience are more highly related to one another for the group of EU countries (all twenty-seven members) than for the global system as a whole. Although *not* measuring the same things, EU measures of ease and salience are related, $r= 0.613$ (with $r^2= 0.375$; $p= 0.0001$). For all 301 borders, $r= 0.185$ (with $r^2= 0.034$; $p= 0.001$). This simple correlation provides some indication that a Deutschian process whereby ease of interaction and salience reinforce each other is indeed occurring (the r^2, or amount of explained variance, is quite high in normal social science findings).

Table 8.2   Comparing EU and World Averages

	Ease of Interaction	**Salience**
World (301 borders)	2.597	1.044
Complete EU		
27 states (34 borders)	2.847	1.137
Original 6 (9 borders)	3.044	1.208
Group Comparisons		
Complete EU and World	t=2.779	t=6.816
	df=333	df=333
	P=0.003	P=0.000
Original 6 and World	t=2.642	t=6.721
	df=308	df=308
	P=0.004	P=0.000

Table 8.3   Tracking Differences in EU Member Groups

	Ease of Interaction	Salience
1952 [9]	3.044	1.208
Original 6		
1973 [2]	2.999	1.152
Denmark		
Ireland		
UK		
1986 [2]	2.346	1.013
Portugal		
Spain		
1995 [3]	2.265	1.033
Austria		
Finland		
Sweden		
2004 [15]	2.894	1.115
Group of 10		
2007 [3]	2.829	1.208
Bulgaria		
Romania		

The second hypothesis above looks within the EU and compares groups of states. It proposes that the original six will have within-EU borders (among themselves and with later joiners) with higher values on the two measures than later groups of joiners. Hypothesis 3 expands this proposition to each successive wave of joiners. Table 8.3 presents some basic descriptive data: the average ease of interaction and salience scores for the seven groupings of joiners that added intra-EU borders (Table 8.1 shows that the 1981 membership of Greece did not add any new intra-EU borders). The averages shown in Table 8.3 are for that group only (e.g., averages for the nine

**Table 8.4   Group Comparisons across
Waves of EU Expansion**

	Ease of Interaction	Salience
Original 6 and Middle	t=1.939	t=3.118
Group (1973, 1986, 1995)	df=14	df=14
	P=0.05	P=0.005
Original 6 and Last 12		
(2004, 2007)	t=0.985	t=1.897
	df=25	df=25
	P=NS	P=0.05
Middle Group and Last 12	t=-2.15	t=-1.638
	df=23	df=23
	P=NS	P=NS

borders generated by the original six, or averages for the fifteen borders generated by the group of ten that joined in 2004). Note that the *highest scores* among all the groups are for the original six, supporting Hypothesis 2. The comparisons provided in Table 8.4 also show that the difference in averages between the original six and other groups (a middle group composed of the 1973, 1986, and 1995 joiners, and the group of the last twelve joiners) are statistically significant. The exception is for the ease of interaction comparison with the last twelve. These comparisons also substantially support Hypothesis 2.

Table 8.3 also shows that members in the 1973, 1986, and 1995 groups each generate continuously lower scores on each measure (except the 1995 group's salience). This supports Hypothesis 3. One interpretation is that as states join, they have had less time for the complex of reciprocal relationships relating to transactions (and between ease of interaction and salience) to take hold. However, Hypothesis 3 is not fully supported. The interpretation noted directly above would not hold for most of the countries joining in 2004. Eight of them were part of the Eastern Bloc—a regional arrangement with economic (and political) networks of its own (the economic organization COMECON). The three Baltic countries were components of a larger state, the USSR, and thus had "internal" borders. The Czech Republic and Slovakia were one state until January 1993. Note that even while the 2004 group reverses the trend of successively lower scores, the average scores on both measures are still lower than those for the original six. The scores are also lower than those of the three countries in the 1973 group. Two of these countries, the UK and Sweden, had also been former members of the European Free Trade Area (or EFTA). Note that Portugal (1986), Austria, and Sweden (1995) had also been members of EFTA. The five former EFTA members thus also brought their own former networks of transactions and interdependence to the EU. The same overall discussion holds for Bulgaria and Romania, which joined the EU in 2007. Although Hypothesis 2, focusing on the original six, is also supported in Table 8.4, Hypothesis 3 is not. There are no significant differences between the last twelve joiners and the eight countries of the middle group.

Conclusion

The findings discussed in Chapter 7 suggested that increased ease of interaction and salience of borders between two countries could represent the dynamics of increased interdependence-integration effects. These findings and propositions were further evaluated in the present chapter, by looking at the expectations this interpretation would suggest for states involved in the processes of integration. The EU, with successive groups of joiners, provided a natural experiment that would allow at least crude tests of this proposed relationship. Hypotheses 1 and 2 found support in the simple statistical comparisons that were conducted. However, Hypothesis 3—that successive waves of joiners would have lower scores on ease of interaction and salience with EU members—was not supported across all the waves of expansion (not holding for the last group of twelve joiners). Although the results produced by looking at the nature of borders are generally supportive, and highly suggestive, in order to address Hypothesis 3 fully, other types of transactions and measures that do exist in the form of time-series data must be investigated.

We have seen in this chapter that the GIS border data have drawbacks that constrain analysis. We have been driven back to a point raised at the very beginning of this book—that time and space must be used together for a full picture or explanation to emerge. Although the GIS data on the nature of borders provided such geographic data as the hypsography (elevation and topographic relief), which is relatively unchanging, it also provided the geo-spatial location of such phenomena as roads, railroads, airfields, military bases, power plants, and so on—features that do change through human enterprise. The problems with using a data set from one time period clearly illustrate the need to create time-series data for such features.

We should also look for other ways to exploit the natural laboratory provided by the EU. Although the analyses presented in this chapter were, in part, a check on the validity of using *the nature of borders* as a surrogate measure for transactions and their place in integration processes, alternative models might exist to explain the findings supporting the first two hypotheses. The findings from alternative geographic or geo-spatial approaches could then be matched against the broadly suggestive findings reported here. For example, one alternative to the use of permeable and salient borders for understanding increased transactions could be the use of "gravity models."

As Walter Isard et al. (1998, 244) note, gravity models are concerned with the frequency and nature of spatial interaction, with a region conceived of as a *mass*. Thus, interregional relations (here, interstate relations) would be seen as interactions among masses, governed by the size of the units and the distance between them: "The frequency of transactions, it has often been suggested, ought to be directly proportional to the product of the masses of the two actors and inversely proportional to the distance, *d*, separating these actors" (Deutsch and Isard 1961, 308). Theoretically, a variety of types of interactions might be investigated, and there might be any number of ways to operationalize mass and distance. With "distance" viewed not simply as kilometers or the existence of a contiguous border but as our index of ease of interaction, would some form of gravity model explain our results? Given that "mass" usually involves some measure of area, demographic or economic size, the answer is "probably not." Recall that dyads with the highest weighted averages for ease of interaction come from the original six members of the EEC. This group includes the dyads composed of the Benelux countries—among the smallest countries in the EEC (and Europe) using almost any economic/demographic/areal measure of size. Despite this plausible consideration, it would still be useful to apply gravity models for comparison to the border measures, using different measures of "mass" and specific types of transactions (such as trade, mail, exchange students, tourism). The waves of EU expansion could more directly be studied, given the availability of data for each country and dyad across time, especially at the time countries joined the EU.

A second alternative was suggested previously, in the discussion of the possible impact of EFTA and COMECON—looking at the effects found in other regions and regional associations. Staying within the Deutschian framework but moving beyond the EU, analyses could be undertaken with the GIS data set looking at the borders of different regional associations or organizations from the late 1980s through the mid-1990s. Comparisons could then be made between different regional organizations and between neighbors that were joint members of regional organizations and those that were not.

Perhaps the best way to evaluate the validity of using the border data as a surrogate for transactions is to use another integration related measure created by Deutsch *within* the European framework. Five decades ago, Richard Savage and Karl Deutsch (1960) developed a means for measuring the relative acceptance (RA) of intergroup transactions. This statistic measures what its name implies, that is, the relative preferences of particular groups for dealing with each other as compared with their respective preferences for dealings with various third parties. In other words, who prefers whom for a partner, in terms of the intensity of their mutual transactions, and contrariwise, who eschews whom? Technically, the relative acceptance statistic weighs positive and negative deviations from a model that assumes that flows of transactions are determined only by the relative activity of interacting units. For example, if Group A accounts for 30 percent of transactions exchanged among a cluster of interacting units, then the model expects that each unit will share 30 percent of its transactions with Group A. The relative acceptance score, or RA, is then computed by comparing expected transactions with actual transactions. Because each unit will actually exchange more or fewer transactions with Group A than the expected 30 percent, the relative preferences of units for dealing (or not dealing) with each other can be imputed.

Examining the actual flows of transactions between and among countries constituted, for Deutsch, an empirical approach to applying theories of interdependence and integration based upon assumptions about communication, closeness, and mutual identification. Following from such theoretical assumptions, and with the relative acceptance statistic devised and available, in the early 1960s Karl Deutsch and his colleagues charted the early course of European integration by analyzing flows of transactions among the peoples of the integrating countries. For example, patterns of relative acceptance scores measuring the international transactions of the 1960s hinted at the partnerships that would become the European Communities and then much later the European Union. What would patterns of transaction flows have shown if Deutsch and his colleagues, or perhaps scholars of a successor generation, had continued their analyses through the entire half century, extending from the 1960s to the present day?

Regrettably, the baseline analyses of the 1960s were never carried forward. Therefore, we do not know what the structures of international transactions, indexed in ways that render them comparable to the 1960s baseline, looked like. One additional direction, therefore, would be to use the RA index on time-series data since the 1960s to track this one measure of transactions across the successive waves of EU expansion (for trade, the flow of labor, and any other type of transaction that involves the movement of goods or people). In addition, measures/indexes similar to the RA index have been developed and could also be used to track the effects of integration within the EU across time. Analyses based on these measures could also then be compared with the analyses based on the RA index.

Note that these alternative analyses move us away from borders per se. But, although they address the task of much more ambitiously testing the theories linking communication, conflict, and integration (the efficacy of which Deutsch's work in the 1960s only hinted), they also provide comparisons that permit us to see the utility of the GIS border data set in dealing with transactions and cooperative behavior.

CHAPTER 9

THE DYNAMISM OF GEOGRAPHY AND GLOBAL POLITICS

I n the first chapter, we began the argument that geography is "inextricably intertwined" with the study of international relations. The two dimensions of time and space were
introduced as the components of the context within which
international relations—or world politics—takes place. We
made the simple point that all theory (and especially theory in
the social sciences) is contingent—hence, the Most and Starr
concept of "nice laws." As such, theory must be sensitive to, and
reflect, the contexts within which it is to work. If theory is to
be the foundation for our view of the world, our propositions
for how the world works, the questions we want to ask about
that world, as well as the research designs to guide our research,
then students of international politics must take context into account. For a full understanding of the international phenomena
we are studying, the temporal dimension is not enough, but
must be combined with the spatial dimension. This is the key
theme that has guided the approach to geopolitics presented
in this book. One reason that the first two chapters introduce
and discuss the work of Harold and Margaret Sprout as well as

that of Kenneth Boulding is because their work makes it easier to see some of the very early connections between geography and international relations, which are at the heart of this book.

A second key theme was to demonstrate in a variety of ways how international relations and spatial/geopolitical factors could be related, in terms of perspective, theory, and empirical research. As these two main themes were being developed and connected, we also saw how geopolitics reflected the multi-disciplinarity required to study international relations. In addition, drawing on a theme I have developed in my own work over the past decade, we saw how geopolitics and its foundation in spatiality required international relations scholars to *cross boundaries*. That is, by including space as well as time, and by relating any entity to its spatial/geopolitical environment (to use the Sproutian terms), we are forced to cross boundaries between levels of analysis, subfields of political science, and whole disciplines. The main tools that were presented for allowing us to do this were the Sprouts' environmental triad, my closely related agent-structure framework of opportunity and willingness, and the interaction opportunity model, which explicitly applied spatial proximity and geopolitical factors to international behavior.

In the second decade of the twenty-first century, much (if not all) of this discussion seems rather self-evident. Why, as noted in Chapter 1, was geography not included in the earliest post–World War II attempts to expand the multidisciplinary nature of international relations? Why did geopolitics need to be reintroduced—if not explicitly rehabilitated—to international relations scholars? As briefly discussed (it could make a whole book on its own!), the presentation and use of geopolitical approaches to international relations found in the late nineteenth century and early twentieth centuries were seen as tainted by ideology, as well as pseudoscientific abuse and misapplication by Nazi ideologues and in Nazi propaganda. In addition, its determinist character during this period permitted it to be neither tested nor falsified and made it easier to use as a matter of ideological "faith."

I have stressed the work of Harold and Margaret Sprout, because a major goal of their work in geopolitics was to rescue it from this previous determinism, and to reintegrate geography into the multidisciplinary study of international relations. I have also stressed their work because their focus on environmental possibilism became a central feature of the "new geopolitics" taken up by geographers (and a smaller number of political scientists) over the past thirty years. This approach, along with environmental probabilism and cognitive behaviorism, was much more congenial to the generally contingent nature of the social sciences, as well as the probabilistic approaches inherent in large-N quantitative statistical studies. Finally, as this book also includes my own scholarly journey as an international relations scholar concerned with context, spatiality, and geo-spatial factors, I have stressed the work of the Sprouts, as it supplied the foundation for opportunity and willingness. As an agent-structure model, opportunity/willingness echoes the triad of entity, environment, and entity-environment relationships. Opportunity/willingness permitted me to address multiple levels of analysis and pull together apparently disparate models, approaches, and research in international conflict into a coherent theoretical structure. Opportunity/willingness also encouraged me (and other scholars) to look at necessary conditions and necessary causal relationships, as well as the more standard studies of causal sufficiency (see, for example, Goertz and Starr 2003). As a foundation, opportunity/willingness both permitted and encouraged its expansion to include key elements of conditionality such as "nice laws" and "substitutability." In sum, the work of the Sprouts in combination with the opportunity/willingness approach provided the framework I have used and have presented in this book to study geopolitics and international relations.

In this book we have also reviewed a number of important applications of spatiality and geography to the study of international relations. We have discussed the concepts of "space" and "distance," relating them to proximity, contiguity, borders, and geographic features—both as constraints on and facilitators of interactions. We have discussed other important elements that make up the environment provided by the international system, such as technology and alliances. Both of these factors affect the impact and meaning of geographical constraints and opportunities. We reviewed work on the diffusion of international phenomena, showing the impact of proximity and borders on the likelihood of conflict and cooperation and the likelihood that conflict will spread (or diffuse) in the system. Proximity, as operationalized by borders, has been found to have such an impact on promoting conflict, that contiguous borders between states are now a standard independent variable in conflict studies, or one that is controlled for while the effects of other variables are being tested. Only some idea of the richness of the research on diffusion, territory, borders, and other geographic factors can be seen in the various overviews provided throughout the book.

We have seen, however, that newer research tools developed by geographers, such as spatial statistics and GIS analytic systems (and the data they can provide), allow us to dig deeper into the relationships between geopolitics and international relations. I have reported at length on the GIS-based data set

I developed on the nature of borders and the research results produced from analyses of that data set. Measuring ease of interaction and salience, these data allow us to go beyond a simple contiguous or noncontiguous coding of the distance between states. Some analyses, such as revisiting earlier findings on diffusion, show that simple contiguity and homeland territory are all we need to understand some of our questions about conflict processes. For some questions it is clear that if territory is involved, then the probability of militarized conflict is increased. However, for other questions, such as whether proximity and borders affect crisis and the escalation of crisis, knowing ease of interaction and salience does make a difference.

Looking at the conditions under which militarized interstate disputes (MIDs) arise, escalate, and spread, the GIS data show that two separate processes tend to be at work and that conflict is most likely when the nature of the borders between states provides both sides with an expected utility for conflict that is greater than no conflict (or a lower-level conflict). The U-shaped finding of Starr and Thomas, reported in Chapter 7, is important in demonstrating that there is not a simple linear relationship between interaction opportunity and conflict, as is captured in most studies by only using contiguity. There is, instead, a low expected utility for conflict when ease of interaction (and salience) is either very low, or very high— thus, the U-shaped relationship. As noted in Chapter 7, these analyses would not have been possible without using GIS or the data generated from the specific GIS used in my studies. It is clear that the potential for studying international relations using various methodologies developed by geographers has barely been tapped and that much more needs to be done.

It is important also to stress that despite living in the highly interdependent, transnational, and globalized world of the twenty-first century, geographic factors such as territory and borders are still integral and meaningful elements of world politics. All humans live (in permanent abodes) on the territory of some state. As with Mark Twain, the reports of the death of the territorial state have been greatly exaggerated. Territory, and the borders that separate states from each other, provide key elements in the structure of the global system—mapping the number and arrangement of the territorial units upon which all humans live. Territory and borders permit a spatial approach to international or global politics, by setting out the location of states and their absolute and relative distances from each other. Borders represent important legal boundaries between states. Such boundaries are just as important (or perhaps even more so) between democracies at peace with one another, who rely on a multitude of economic and social transactions, as they are to adversaries who "securitize" their borders with fortifications and military capabilities. Borders continue to act as factors of constraint on human interaction, as well as factors that facilitate human interaction. Territory and borders have significant effects on international relations, because of their *meaning* to humans (whether scholars, policy makers, or peoples). There is a deep connection between individuals, and groups of people, to the territory they live on and the territory that their ancestors lived on. What is so important to the identity and cohesion of groups, thus also can become one of the major obstacles in managing and resolving conflict between those groups. We have argued that geography is "dynamic" in that the *meaning* of territory, distance, and borders can change (and quite rapidly) in the perceptions of peoples and foreign policy–making elites. This can be done through technology, or as argued in this book, through alliances. Both the internal and external politics of peoples, substate organizations, and states affect the creation, dissolution, and meaning of borders. In sum, even in the world of growing interdependence and globalization, territory and borders have important roles to play in the reality of, and study of, international relations.

In the first chapter I discussed Bobrow's two hypothetical visits to the international relations section of a library. During neither of those visits could work on geography be found. That would not be the case today. As can be seen from the discussions and citations in this book, geography and geopolitics would be well represented in the work of political scientists and geographers alike. Not only would geography be present, but works drawing on, and drawing our attention to, spatial and geopolitical factors would highlight important connections between IR and all aspects of the environment and the attendant growth in environmental studies. The same could be said for the complementary scholarly endeavors addressing peace studies and conflict analysis. Although the presence of such works in our current libraries may be seen as new, they, too, were introduced decades ago by scholars such as the Sprouts and Boulding. In part, this book is a tribute to their work and their place in the complex relationship between geopolitics and international relations.

Notes

Chapter One

1. See Most and Starr (1989), especially their discussions of "nice laws" and "substitutability."

2. My colleagues and I used these interests and approaches most recently to investigate both internal conflict and cross-border conflict of the Israeli conflict system (Starr et al. 2011).

3. William T. R. Fox, in elaborating on the Sprouts' possibilism, has noted that "Harold and Margaret Sprout are the American political scientists with the most sustained interest in and influence on geopolitical thinking from the 1930's to the 1970's" (1985, 27).

4. Note also the work of Hoffman and Aleprete (2009), which shows, in addition to how greater interaction opportunities might lead to conflict, how conflict between contiguous states could lead to greater interaction opportunities.

Chapter Two

1. Thus, the historical tradition that would investigate topics such as Franco-Prussian relations between 1871 and 1914 was often simply replaced with the analysis of some correlate of war (such as alliance formation or system polarity) between 1816 and 1965, the original time period covered by the data sets created by the Correlates of War Project.

2. O'Loughlin and Anselin (1992, 16) note that "Giddens prefers the term *locale* over place because place suggests a spatial container while locale is the setting of interaction and the contextuality of social life." In earlier work, I have also used Giddens in this way, preferring the broader idea of context over more narrow meanings such as "container."

3. See, for instance, the work of Agnew, or that of David Newman (e.g., 1991, 1996).

4. A good example of the function of space and spatiality in the "operation of any social operation" is found in the fascinating "Sugarscape" simulation presented in Epstein and Axtell (1996). The "agent-based" computer modeling methodology presented by Epstein and Axtell puts spatial distribution at the heart of a multidisciplinary model of how societies develop, grow, become more complex, and die.

5. See also Quincy Wright's classic *A Study of War* to see how he conceived of various types of social distance between states or policy makers. In his massive work searching for the causes of war, Wright (1942, 1240) hypothesized that the greater the "distance" between states, the greater the probability of war—"when powers are so isolated from one another that there is no basis for mutual understanding." He attempted to measure distance through the many forms of physical and psychological distances that exist between social units—technological and strategic, intellectual and legal, social and political, psychic and expectancy, and policy distances.

6. According to Cahill (1998) in *The Gifts of the Jews,* this "Western" notion of time stems from the Judeo-Christian tradition, first devised by the Jews of the Old Testament who "invented history." The Old Testament was written in "real" "historical" terms, breaking out of the existing cyclical and eternal views of time held by other peoples and religions.

7. Kissinger comments on Chinese self-perception: "Chinese elites grew accustomed to the notion that China was unique—not just 'a great civilization' among others, but civilization itself" (2011, 10).

8. Abler et al. (1971, 82–83) use the following formula to calculate time-space convergence:

$$TT1–TT2 \div Y2–Y1$$

where TT1 and TT2 are the travel times between two places at two different times, and Y1 and Y2 are the two dates in question.

9. See, for example, the work of Barry Smith (2001; Smith and Varzi 2000).

10. Anselin has been one of the pioneers in the development of spatial econometrics as well as variants such as ESDA. A brief description of spatial data analysis is provided by Goodchild et al.: "Principles of statistics in a spatial context are contained in spatial statistics, geostatistics, and spatial econometrics and based on the concept of a spatial random field. They incorporate models of spatial dependence and spatial heterogeneity, allowing for specification testing, estimation, and prediction of spatial phenomena observed as points, continuous surfaces, or lattices (regions)" (2000, 148).

Chapter Three

1. See also Bruce Bueno de Mesquita's (1989) focus on "progress" in a Lakatosian sense.

2. Although the border data set created by Starr and Most (1976) predated the first available data set from the Correlates of War Project, the CWP has developed, and continually updated, the most extensive and complete data set on borders available for international systemic actors. The data set covers borders since 1816, including all states as well as colonies and other territories. Go to www.correlatesofwar.org/datasets. htm.

3. Although Vasquez (1996) has provided three theoretical perspectives linking geography and conflict, they also reduce to Diehl's two views. Vasquez's "territoriality perspective" discusses geography as a source of conflict, something that states fight over. His two other perspectives—"proximity perspective" and "interaction perspective"—fall under Diehl's rubric of geography as a "facilitating condition." Vasquez's proximity perspective is about the ease with which states can reach each other militarily, and the interaction perspective links closeness or proximity to the frequency of interaction.

4. See, for example, Morton and Starr (2001) for a discussion of "elite powers" that combine large land armies with large navies or strategic bombers and missiles.

Chapter Four

1. For example, according to the 1933 Montevideo Convention, Article I, "The State as a person of international law should possess the following qualifications: (a) a permanent population; (b) a defined territory; (c) a government; and (d) the capacity to enter into relations with other states." It is important that territory must be "defined"—thus the importance of borders (see Bederman 2001).

2. These agreements became part of the EU legal framework in 1999, through a protocol to the Treaty of Amsterdam.

Chapter Five

1. Although we will briefly review some of the reasons states enter into alliances, it should be clear that this is not the purpose of our discussion.

2. Goertz (1989, 5) forcefully presents a similar position: "The fundamental characteristic of contextual indicators is that they are attentive to the shifting meaning of a concept in different environments and thereby generate more valid indicators for general concepts. Likewise, we speak of a contextual theory where the relationship between variables is not just additive, but where the importance of effects of the different variables are theorized to be different in different environments."

3. The initial data-collection period of the Correlates of War Project.

4. States may also join alliances to control allies (including the maintenance of the governments of allies), to legitimate in their domestic political arenas unilateral activities such as intervention, for a variety of collective goods (stability, order, deterrence) or private goods (economic or military aid, help against a specific opponent, to maintain domestic control).

Chapter Six

1. The notion that changes in bordering areas create uncertainty because of their proximity was based on arguments developed by Midlarsky (1970, 1975) and applied in Most and Starr (1980).

2. This research project was supported by a University of South Carolina Research and Productive Scholarship Award (No. 13570-E120), which in turn was instrumental in securing a National Science Foundation grant (SBR-9731056) to continue the project.

3. Data for this project are from the Digital Chart of the World (DCW), produced by ESRI for the Defense Mapping Agency in 1992. The data contained in the DCW were derived primarily from maps in the Defense Mapping Agency Operational Navigation Chart series that were used to generate a 1:1,000,000-scale vector database, covering the entire surface of the earth. One major (perhaps "heroic") assumption of the project is that the border data generated by the 1992 DCW can be usefully applied backward for twenty to twenty-five years and forward for ten to fifteen years. That is, the data retain validity as a rough surrogate for the ease of interaction and salience of areas for this time frame.

4. List of data layers in the ARC/INFO Digital Chart of the World: Political and Oceans; Populated Place; Railroads; Roads; Utilities; Drainage; Drainage Supplemental; Hypsography; Hypsography Supplemental; Ocean Features; Physiography; Aeronautical; Cultural Landmark; Transportation Structure; Vegetation; Land Cover. A seventeenth layer, the Data Quality layer, provides information on the particular source of data for a given tile and when that source was last updated.

5. One of the more useful aspects of GIS systems is the ability to create *any size* "buffer" on either side of a border. It should be noted that the original tests and analyses were performed on Israel. Given Israel's size, a 10,000-meter buffer on each side of the border seemed appropriate. However, after other test-case analyses, it was decided to use a 50,000-meter buffer.

6. The Opportunity for Interaction/Ease of Interaction index, with its four-category scheme, was developed as follows. Although only one combination of variables leads to a category 4 designation, note how different combinations may compose each of the other categories:

4=presence of a road and the presence of a railroad and low slope

3=a road or a railroad and low slope

3=a road and a railroad and medium slope

3=no road, no railroad, and low slope

2=a road or a railroad and medium slope

2=a road and a railroad and high slope

2=a road or a railroad and high slope
1=no road, no railroad, and medium slope
1=no road, no railroad, and high slope

Chapter Seven

1. Consequently, for this analysis we have sixty-one usable conflict dyads as opposed to the twenty-seven for Huth and twenty-two for Goertz and Diehl.

2. This results in sixty-five total cases: forty-eight contiguous, seven near-neighbor, and ten distant cases of crisis. Due to the relatively small number of cases, the near-neighbor and distant cases of crisis have been combined.

3. Therefore, the forty-eight contiguous cases have been divided into two groups based on whether each observation falls in the first through third quartiles or fourth quartile for the variable in question (the fourth quartile having the *greatest* ease of interaction, or salience, or "vitalness," or length of border).

4. For a full description of the analyses, see Starr and Thomas (2005).

REFERENCES

Abler, Ronald, John S. Adams, and Peter Gould. 1971. *Spatial Organization: The Geographer's View of the World.* Englewood Cliffs, NJ: Prentice Hall.

Agnew, John A., and James S. Duncan. 1989. "Introduction." In *The Power of Place,* ed. John A. Agnew and James S. Duncan, 1–8. Boston, MA: Unwin Hyman.

Akerman, James R., ed. 2009. *The Imperial Map.* Chicago: University of Chicago Press.

Anselin, Luc. 1999. "The Future of Spatial Analysis in the Social Sciences." *Geographic Information Sciences* 5: 67–76.

Bederman, David J. 2001. *International Law Frameworks.* New York: Foundation Press.

Bernauer, T., T. Böhmelt, H. Buhaug, N. P. Gleditsch, T. Tribaldos, E. B. Weibust, and G. Wischnath. 2012. "Water-Related Intrastate Conflict and Cooperation (WARICC): A New Event Dataset." *International Interactions* 38: 529–545.

Berry, B. J. L. 1969. "A Synthesis of Formal and Functional Regions Using a General Field Theory of Spatial Behavior." In *Spatial Analysis,* ed. B. J. L. Berry and D. F. Marble, 419–428. Englewood Cliffs, NJ: Prentice Hall.

Bobrow, Davis. 1972. *International Relations, New Approaches.* New York: Free Press.

Boulding, Kenneth E. 1962. *Conflict and Defense.* New York: Harper and Row.

Boyce, David E., and Ronald Miller. 2011. "In Memoriam: Walter Isard (1919–2010)." *Journal of Regional Science* 51: 1–4.

Braithwaite, A. 2005. "Location, Location, Location... Identifying Hot Spots of International Conflict." *International Interactions* 31: 251–273.

———. 2006. "The Geographic Spread of Militarized Disputes." *Journal of Peace Research* 43: 507–522.

Braumoeller, Bear. 2003. "Causal Complexity and the Study of Politics." *Political Analysis* 11: 209–233.

Brecher, Michael, and Jonathan Wilkenfeld. 1997. *A Study of Crisis.* Ann Arbor: University of Michigan Press.

Bremer, Stuart A. 1992. "Dangerous Dyads: Conditions Affecting the Likelihood of Interstate War, 1816–1965." *Journal of Conflict Resolution* 36: 309–341.

Brochmann, Marit, Jan Ketil Rod, and Nils Petter Gleditsch. 2012. "International Borders and Conflict Revisited." *Conflict Management and Peace Science* 29: 170–194.

Bubalo, Anthony, and Malcolm Cook. 2010. "Horizontal Asia." *The American Interest* 5(5): 12–19.

Bueno de Mesquita, Bruce. 1981. *The War Trap*. New Haven, CT: Yale University Press.

———. 1989. "The Contribution of Expected-Utility Theory to the Study of International Conflict." In *Handbook of War Studies,* ed. Manus I. Midlarsky, 143–169. Boston, MA: Unwin Hyman.

Buhaug, Halvard, Scott Gates, and P. Lujala. 2009. "Geography, Rebel Capability, and the Duration of Civil Conflict." *Journal of Conflict Resolution* 53: 544–569.

Cahill, Thomas. 1998. *The Gifts of the Jews*. New York: Doubleday.

Choucri, Nazli, and Robert C. North. 1975. *Nations in Conflict*. San Francisco, CA: W. H. Freeman.

Christin, Thomas, and Simon Hug. 2012. "Federalism, the Geographic Location of Groups, and Conflict." *Conflict Management and Peace Science* 29: 93–122.

Cioffi-Revilla, Claudio, and Harvey Starr. 1995. "Opportunity, Willingness, and Political Uncertainty: Theoretical Foundations of Politics." *Journal of Theoretical Politics* 7(4): 447–476.

Cobb, Roger W., and Charles Elder. 1970. *International Community: A Regional and Global Study*. New York: Holt, Rinehart, Winston.

Cohen, Saul. 1963. *Geography and Politics in a World Divided*. New York: Random House.

Collier, David. 1993. "The Comparative Method." In *Political Science: The State of the Discipline II,* ed. Ada W. Finifter, 105–119. Washington, DC: The American Political Science Association.

Cowen, David J. 1990. "GIS versus CAD versus DBMS: What Are the Differences?" In *Introductory Readings in Geographic Information Systems,* ed. D. J. Peuquet and D. F. Marble, 52–62. London: Taylor and Francis.

Deutsch, Karl W. 1966. "External Influences on the Internal Behavior of States." In *Approaches to Comparative and International Politics,* ed. R. Barry Farrell, 5–26. Evanston, IL: Northwestern University Press.

Deutsch, Karl W., et al. 1957. *Political Community and the North Atlantic Area*. Princeton, NJ: Princeton University Press.

Deutsch, Karl W., et al. 1967. *France, Germany, and the Western Alliance*. New York: Scribner's.

Deutsch, Karl W., and Walter Isard. 1961. "A Note on a Generalized Concept of Effective Distance." *Behavioral Science* 6: 308–311.

Diehl, Paul F. 1991. "Geography and War: A Review and Assessment of the Empirical Literature." *International Interactions* 17: 11–27.

———. 1999. "Territory and International Conflict: An Overview." In *A Road Map to War,* ed. Paul F. Diehl, viii–xx. Nashville, TN: Vanderbilt University Press.

Dougherty, James E., and Robert L. Pfaltzgraff. 1990. *Contending Theories of International Relations,* 3rd ed. New York: Harper and Row.

Environmental Systems Research Institute [ESRI]. 1992. *ARC/INFO: GIS Today and Tomorrow.* New York: ESRI.

Epstein, Joshua M., and Robert Axtell. 1996. *Growing Artificial Societies.* Cambridge, MA: MIT Press.

Falah, G., and David Newman. 1995. "The Spatial Manifestation of Threat: Israelis and Palestinians Seek a 'Good' Border." *Political Geography* 14: 689–706.

Flint, Colin. 2012. "Peace Science as Normal Science: What Role for Geography in the Coming Revolution?" In *What Do We Know About War?,* 2nd ed., ed. John Vasquez, 291–300. Lanham, MD: Rowman and Littlefield.

Fox, William T. R. 1985. "Geopolitics and International Relations." In *On Geopolitics: Classical and Nuclear,* ed. C. E. Zoppo and C. Zorgbibe, 15–44. Boston, MA: Martinus Nijhoff.

Friedman, Gil. 2002. "Toward a Spatial Model of Protracted Conflict Management: The Palestinian Case." PhD diss., University of South Carolina.

Friedman, Gil, and Harvey Starr. 1997. *Agency, Structure, and International Politics.* London: Routledge.

Furlong, K., N. P. Gleditsch, and H. Hegre. 2006. "Geographic Opportunity and Neomathusian Willingness: Boundaries, Shared Rivers, and Conflict." *International Interactions* 32: 79–108.

Galton, Antony. 2001. "Space, Time, and the Representation of Geographical Reality." *Topoi* 20: 173–187.

Garnham, David. 1976. "Power Parity and Lethal International Violence, 1969–1973." *Journal of Conflict Resolution* 20: 379–394.

Gibler, D. 2007. "Bordering on Peace: Democracy, Territorial Issues, and Conflict." *International Studies Quarterly* 51: 509–532.

Gibler, Douglas M., and Jaroslav Tir. 2010. "Settled Borders and Regime Type: Democratic Transitions as Consequences of Peaceful Territorial Transfers." *American Journal of Political Science* 5: 951–968.

Giddens, A. 1984. *The Constitution of Society.* Berkeley: University of California Press.

Glassner, M. J. 1992. *Political Geography.* New York: Wiley.

Gleditsch, Kristian S. 2002. *All International Politics Is Local.* Ann Arbor: University of Michigan Press.

Gleditsch, Kristian S., and Michael D. Ward. 2001. "Measuring Space: A Minimum Distance Database." *Journal of Peace Research* 38: 739–758.

Gleditsch, Kristian Skrede, and Nils B. Weidmann. 2012. "Richardson in the Information Age: GIS and Spatial Data in International Studies." *Annual Reviews of Political Science* 15: 461–481.

Gleditsch, Nils Petter. 1969. "The International Airline Network: A Test of the Zipf and Stouffer Hypotheses." *Peace Research Society: Papers* 11: 123–153.

Gleditsch, Nils Petter, and J. David Singer. 1975. "Distance and International War, 1816–1995." In *Proceedings of the International Peace Research Association,* 481–506. Oslo, Norway.

Goertz, Gary. 1989. "Contextual Theories and Indicators in World Politics." Center for International Economic History, University of Geneva.

Goertz, Gary, and Paul F. Diehl. 1992. *Territorial Changes and International Conflict*. London: Routledge.

———. 1993. "Enduring Rivalries: Theoretical Constructs and Empirical Patterns." *International Studies Quarterly* 37: 147–171.

———. 1995. "Taking 'Enduring' Out of Enduring Rivalry: The Rivalry Approach to War and Peace." *International Interactions* 21: 291–308.

Goertz, Gary, and Harvey Starr, eds. 2003. *Necessary Conditions*. Lanham, MD: Rowman and Littlefield.

Goodchild, Michael F., Luc Anselin, Richard P. Appelbaum, and Barbara Herr Harthorn. 2000. "Toward Spatially Integrated Social Science." *International Regional Science Review* 23: 139–159.

Gray, Colin. 1977. *The Geopolitics of the Nuclear Era*. New York: Crane Russak.

Green, Elliott. 2012. "On the Size and Shape of African States." *International Studies Quarterly* 56: 229–244.

Haas, Ernst. 1958. *The Uniting of Europe*. Stanford, CA: Stanford University Press.

Hallberg, Johan Dittrich. 2012. "PRIO Conflict Site 1989–2008: A Geo-Referenced Dataset on Armed Conflict." *Conflict Management and Peace Science* 29 (April 2012): 219–223.

Hammarstrom, Mats, and Birger Heldt. 2002. "The Diffusion of Military Intervention: Testing a Network Position Approach." *International Interactions* 28: 355–377.

Hensel, Paul R. 2000. "Territory: Theory and Evidence on Geography and Conflict." In *What Do We Know About War?* ed. John A. Vasquez, 57–84. Boulder, CO: Rowman and Littlefield.

———. 2001. "Contentious Issues and World Politics: The Management of Territorial Claims in the Americas, 1816–1992." *International Studies Quarterly* 45: 81–109.

———. 2012. "Territory: Geography, Contentious Issues, and World Politics." In *What Do We Know About War?*, 2nd edition, ed. John Vasquez, 291–300. Lanham, MD: Rowman and Littlefield.

Herz, John. 1957. "The Rise and Demise of the Territorial State." *World Politics* 9: 473–493.

———. 1968. "The Territorial State Revisited: Reflections on the Nature of the Nation-State." *Polity* 1: 11–34.

Hoffman, A. A., and M. E. Aleprete. 2009. "Political Arrangements and Geographic Proximity: The Effect(s) of Interstate Conflict on Land Borders." Paper presented at the Annual Meeting of the International Studies Association, New York, February.

Holsti, K. J. 1991. *Peace and War: Armed Conflicts and International Order, 1648–1989*. Cambridge: Cambridge University Press.

Huth, Paul. 1996. *Standing Your Ground: Territorial Disputes and International Conflict*. Ann Arbor: University of Michigan Press.

Huth, Paul, and Todd Allee. 2002. *The Democratic Peace and Territorial Conflict in the Twentieth Century*. Ann Arbor: University of Michigan Press.

Hyndman, Jennifer. 2012. "Geopolitics of Migration and Mobility." *GEOpolitics* 17: 243–255.

Isard, Walter, et al. 1998. *Methods of Interregional and Regional Analysis.* Aldershot, UK: Ashgate.

Job, Brian. 1981. "Grins Without Cats: In Pursuit of Knowledge of International Alliances." In *Cumulation in International Relations,* ed. P. T. Hopmann et al., 39–63. Denver, CO: University of Denver Monograph Series in World Affairs.

Kacowicz, Arie M. 1994. "The Problem of Peaceful Territorial Change." *International Studies Quarterly* 38: 219–254.

Keohane, Robert O. 1984. *After Hegemony.* Princeton, NJ: Princeton University Press.

Keohane, Robert O., and Joseph S. Nye, eds. 1972. *Transnational Relations and World Politics.* Cambridge, MA: Harvard University Press.

Keohane, Robert O., and Joseph S. Nye. 1977. *Power and Interdependence.* Glenview, IL: Scott Foresman.

Kirby, Andrew, and Michael D. Ward. 1987. "Space, Spatiality, Geography, Territoriality, Context, Locale—and Conflict." Paper presented at the annual meeting of the American Political Science Association, Chicago, September.

Kissinger, Henry. 2011. *On China.* New York: Penguin.

Kobrin, Stephen J. 1997. "Transnational Integration, National Markets, and Nation-States." In *International Business: An Emerging Vision,* ed. Brian Toyne and Douglas Nigh, 242–256. Columbia: University of South Carolina Press.

Krasner, Stephen, ed. 1983. *International Regimes.* Ithaca, NY: Cornell University Press.

Kuhn, Thomas S. 1962. *The Structure of Scientific Revolutions.* Chicago: University of Chicago Press.

Lave, Charles A., and James G. March. 1975. *An Introduction to Models in the Social Sciences.* New York: Harper and Row.

Leeds, Brett Ashley. 2003. "Do Alliances Deter Aggression? The Influence of Military Alliances on the Initiation of Militarized Interstate Disputes." *American Journal of Political Science* 47: 427–439.

Leeds, Brett Ashley, and David R. Davis. 1999. "Beneath the Surface: Regime Type and International Interaction, 1953–1978." *Journal of Peace Research* 36: 5–21.

Lemke, Douglas. 1995. "The Tyranny of Distance: Redefining Relevant Dyads." *International Interactions* 21(1): 23–38.

Lemke, Douglas, and William Reed. 2001. "The Relevance of Politically Relevant Dyads." *Journal of Conflict Resolution* 45(1): 126–144.

Levy, Jack S. 2000. "Loss Aversion, Framing Effects, and International Conflict: Perspectives from Prospect Theory." In *Handbook of War Studies II,* ed. Manus I. Midlarsky, 193–221. Ann Arbor: University of Michigan Press.

Maoz, Zeev. 1996. *Domestic Sources of Global Change.* Ann Arbor: University of Michigan Press.

———. 2010. *Networks of Nations: The Evolution, Structure, and Impact of International Networks, 1816–2001.* New York: Cambridge University Press.

———. 2012. "How Network Analysis Can Inform the Study of International Relations." *Conflict Management and Peace Science* 29: 247–256.

Maoz, Zeev, and Bruce Russett. 1992. "Alliance, Contiguity, Wealth, and Political Stability: Is the Lack of Conflict Among Democracies a Statistical Artifact?" *International Interactions* 17: 245–267.

Marble, D. F. 1990. "Geographic Information Systems: An Overview." In *Introductory Readings in Geographic Information Systems,* ed. D. J. Peuquet and D. F. Marble, 8–17. London: Taylor and Francis.

Midlarsky, Manus I. 1970. "Mathematical Models of Instability and a Theory of Diffusion." *International Studies Quarterly* 14: 60–84.

———. 1975. *On War.* New York: Free Press.

Mitchell, Sara McLaughlin, and Brandon C. Prins. 1999. "Beyond Territorial Contiguity: Issues at Stake in Democratic Militarized Interstate Disputes." *International Studies Quarterly* 43: 169–183.

Monmonier, Mark. 1991. *How to Lie with Maps.* Chicago: University of Chicago Press.

Morton, Jeffrey S., and Harvey Starr. 2001. "Uncertainty, Change, and War: Power Fluctuations and War in the Modern Elite Power System." *Journal of Peace Research* 38: 49–66.

Most, Benjamin A., and Harvey Starr. 1980. "Diffusion, Reinforcement, Geopolitics, and the Spread of War." *American Political Science Review* 74: 932–946.

———. 1989. *Inquiry, Logic and International Politics.* Columbia: University of South Carolina Press.

Most, Benjamin, Harvey Starr, and Randolph Siverson. 1989. "The Logic and Study of the Diffusion of International Conflict." In *Handbook of War Studies,* ed. Manus Midlarsky, 111–139. Boston, MA: Unwin Hyman.

Newman, David. 1991. "On Writing 'Involved' Political Geography." *Political Geography Quarterly* 10: 195–199.

———. 1996. "Writing Together Separately: Critical Discourse and the Problems of Cross-Ethnic Co-Authorship." *Area* 28: 1–12.

———. 1999. "Real Spaces, Symbolic Spaces: Interrelated Notions of Territory in the Arab-Israeli Conflict." In *A Road Map to War,* ed. Paul Diehl, 3–34. Nashville, TN: Vanderbilt University Press.

———. 2006a. "Borders and Bordering: Towards an Interdisciplinary Dialogue." *European Journal of Social Theory* 9: 171–186.

———. 2006b. "The Lines That Continue to Separate Us: Borders in Our 'Borderless' World." *Progress in Human Geography* 30: 1–19.

Nicholson, Michael. 1989. *Formal Theories in International Relations.* Cambridge: Cambridge University Press.

Nijman, Jan. 1991. "The Dynamics of Superpower Spheres of Influence: U.S. and Soviet Military Activities, 1948–1978." *International Interactions* 17: 63–91.

O'Loughlin, John. 1987. "The Contribution of Political Geography to the Study of International Conflicts: A Research Agenda." Paper presented at the annual meeting of the American Political Science Association, Chicago, September.

O'Loughlin, John, and Luc Anselin. 1992. "Geography of International Conflict and

Cooperation: Theory and Methods." In *The New Geopolitics,* ed. Michael Don Ward, 11–38. Philadelphia, PA: Gordon and Breach.

Østerud, Ø. 1988. "The Uses and Abuses of Geopolitics." *Journal of Peace Research* 25: 191–199.

Ostrom, Elinor. 1990. *Governing the Commons.* Cambridge: Cambridge University Press.

O'Sullivan, Patrick. 1986. *Geopolitics.* New York: St. Martin's Press.

Owsiak, Andrew P. 2012. "Signing Up for Peace: International Boundary Agreements, Democracy, and Militarized Interstate Conflict." *International Studies Quarterly* 56: 51–66.

Peuquet, D. J., and D. F. Marble. 1990. "ARC/INFO: An Example of a Contemporary Geographic Information System." In *Introductory Readings in Geographic Information Systems,* ed. D. J. Peuquet, and D. F. Marble, 90–99. London: Taylor and Francis.

Prescott, J. R. V. 1987. *Political Frontiers and Boundaries.* London: Allen and Unwin.

Pruitt, Dean G., and Sung Hee Kim. 2004. *Social Conflict: Escalation, Stalemate, and Settlement.* Boston, MA: McGraw-Hill.

Raleigh, C., A. Linke, H. Hegre, and J. Karlsen. 2010. "Introducing ACLED: An Armed Conflict Location and Event Dataset." *Journal of Peace Research* 47: 1–10.

Rosenau, James N. 1980. "The Adaptation of National Societies: A Theory of Political Behavior and Transformation." In *The Scientific Study of Foreign Policy,* rev. ed., ed. J. N. Rosenau, 501–534. London: Frances Pinter.

Russett, Bruce M. 1967. *International Regions and the International System.* Chicago: Rand McNally.

———. 1974. "Transactions, Community, and International Political Integration." In *Power and Community in World Politics,* ed. B. M. Russett, 325–345. San Francisco, CA: W. H. Freeman.

Russett, Bruce M., and John R. Oneal. 2001. *Triangulating Peace.* New York: W.W. Norton and Company.

Sack, R. D. 1986. *Human Territoriality.* Cambridge: Cambridge University Press.

Sample, Susan G. 2002. "The Outcomes of Military Buildups: Minor States vs. Major Powers." *Journal of Peace Research* 39: 669–691.

Savage, Richard, and Karl W. Deutsch. 1960. "A Statistical Model of the Gross Analysis of Transaction Flows." *Econometrica* 28: 551–572.

Singer, J. David. 1961. "The Relevance of the Behavioral Sciences to the Study of International Relations." *Behavioral Science* 6: 324–325.

Siverson, Randolph M., and Harvey Starr. 1991. *The Diffusion of War.* Ann Arbor: University of Michigan Press.

Sloan, G. R. 1988. *Geopolitics in United States Strategic Policy, 1890–1987.* New York: St. Martin's Press.

Smith, Barry. 2001. "Fiat Objects." *Topoi* 20: 131–148.

Smith, Barry, and A. C. Varzi. 2000. "Fiat and Bona Fide Boundaries." *Philosophy and Phenomenological Research* 60: 401–420.

Snyder, Glenn. 1984. "The Security Dilemma in Alliance Politics." *World Politics* 36: 461–495.

Snyder, Richard C., H. W. Bruck, and Burton Sapin. 1954. *Decision-Making as an Approach to the Study of International Politics*. Foreign Policy Analysis Project. Princeton University.

Sprout, Harold. 1963. "Geopolitical Hypotheses in Technological Perspective." *World Politics* 15: 187–212.

Sprout, Harold, and Margaret Sprout. 1965. *The Ecological Perspective on Human Affairs*. Princeton, NJ: Princeton University Press.

———. 1969. "Environmental Factors in the Study of International Politics." In *International Politics and Foreign Policy,* ed. James N. Rosenau, 41–56. New York: Free Press.

———. 1971. *Towards a Politics of the Planet Earth*. New York: Van Nostrand Reinhold.

Starr, Harvey. 1978. "'Opportunity' and 'Willingness' as Ordering Concepts in the Study of War." *International Interactions* 4: 363–387.

———. 1991. "Democratic Dominoes: Diffusion Approaches to the Spread of Democracy in the International System." *Journal of Conflict Resolution* 35: 356–381.

———. 1997. *Anarchy, Order, and Integration*. Ann Arbor: University of Michigan Press.

———. 2000. "Using Geographic Information Systems to Revisit Enduring Rivalries: The Case of Israel." *Geopolitics* 5: 37–56.

———. 2002a. "Opportunity, Willingness and Geographic Information Systems: Reconceptualizing Borders in International Relations." *Political Geography* 21: 243–261.

———. 2002b. "Cumulation, Synthesis and Research Design for the 'Post-Fourth Wave.'" In *Millennium Reflections on International Studies,* ed. Michael Brecher and Frank Harvey, 361–373. Ann Arbor: University of Michigan Press.

———, ed. 2006. *Approaches, Levels, and Methods of Analysis in International Politics: Crossing Boundaries*. New York: Palgrave Macmillan.

Starr, Harvey, Roger Liu, and G. Dale Thomas. 2011. "The Geography of Conflict: Using GIS to Analyze Israel's External and Internal Conflict Systems." Paper presented at the "New Horizons in Conflict System Analysis: Applications to the Middle East—a Cross-Disciplinary Conference at the University of South Carolina," University of South Carolina, Columbia, October.

Starr, Harvey, and Benjamin A. Most. 1976. "The Substance and Study of Borders in International Relations Research." *International Studies Quarterly* 20: 581–620.

Starr, Harvey, and G. Dale Thomas. 2002. "The 'Nature' of Contiguous Borders: Ease of Interaction, Salience, and the Analysis of Crisis." *International Interactions* 28: 213–235.

———. 2005. "The Nature of Borders and International Conflict: Revisiting Hypotheses on Territory." *International Studies Quarterly* 49: 123–139.

Thies, Cameron G. 2001. "Territorial Nationalism in Spatial Rivalries." *International Interactions* 27(4): 399–441.

Tir, Jaroslav, and Douglas M. Stinnett. 2011. "The Institutional Design of Riparian Treaties: The Role of River Issues." *Journal of Conflict Resolution* 55: 606–631.

Tollefsen, A. F., H. Strand, and H. Buhaug. 2012. "PRIO-GRID: A Unified Spatial Data Structure." *Journal of Peace Research* 49: 363–374.

Vanzo, John P. 1999. "Border Configuration and Conflict: Geographical Compactness as a Territorial Ambition of States." In *A Road Map to War,* ed. Paul Diehl, 73–112. Nashville, TN: Vanderbilt University Press.

Vasquez, John A. 1993. *The War Puzzle.* Cambridge: Cambridge University Press.
———. 1996. "Distinguishing Rivals That Go to War from Those That Do Not: A Quantitative Comparative Case Study of the Two Paths to War." *International Studies Quarterly* 40: 531–558.

Vasquez, John A., and Paul D. Senese. 2003. "A Unified Explanation of Territorial Conflict: Testing the Impact of Sampling Bias, 1919–1992." *International Studies Quarterly* 47: 275–298.

Walt, Stephen. 1985. "Alliance Formation and the Balance of Power." *International Security* 9: 3–43.

Ward, Michael D. 1982. *Research Gaps in Alliance Dynamics.* Denver, CO: University of Denver Monograph Series in World Affairs.
———. 1991. "Introduction: Throwing the State Back Out." In *The New Geopolitics,* ed. Michael Don Ward, 1–10. Philadelphia: Gordon and Breach.

Wesley, J. P. 1962. "Frequency of Wars and Geographical Opportunity." *Journal of Conflict Resolution* 6: 387–389.

Wood, W. 2000. "GIS as a Tool for Territorial Negotiations." *IBRU Boundary and Security Bulletin* 7: 79–108.

Wright, Quincy. 1942. *A Study of War.* Chicago: University of Chicago Press.

Zinnes, Dina. 1976. "The Problem of Cumulation." In *In Search of Global Patterns,* ed. James Rosenau, 161–166. New York: Free Press.

Zipf, G. K. 1949. *Human Behavior and the Principle of Least Effort.* Cambridge, MA: Addison-Wesley.

CREDITS

I have drawn upon a number of my published works in writing significant sections of various chapters: "Joining Political and Geographic Perspectives: Geopolitics and International Relations," *International Interactions* 17 (1991): 1–9; "The Power of Place and the Future of Spatial Analysis in the Study of Conflict," *Conflict Management and Peace Science* 20 (2003): 1–20; "Territory, Proximity, and Spatiality: The Geography of International Conflict," *International Studies Review* 7 (2005): 387–406; "International Borders: What They Are, What They Mean, and Why We Should Care," *SAIS Review* 26 (2006): 3–10; "Alliances and Geopolitics," *Political Geography Quarterly* 9 (1990): 232–248 (with Randolph Siverson); "Opportunity, Willingness and Geographic Information Systems: Reconceptualizing Borders in International Relations," *Political Geography* 21 (2002): 243–261; "The Nature of Borders and Conflict: Revisiting Hypotheses on Territory and War," *International Studies Quarterly* 49 (2005): 123–139 (with Dale Thomas); "The 'Nature' of Contiguous Borders: Ease of Interaction, Salience, and the Analysis of Crisis," *International Interactions* 28 (2002): 213–231 (with Dale Thomas).

I gratefully acknowledge these journals and coauthors and thank them for their permission to draw upon this work in this book.

INDEX

Abler, Ronald, 20–21, 22, 23, 26, 28–31, 33, 162n8
absolute distance, 7, 25, 26, 27–28, 35, 43–44, 78, 83, 88
absolute location, 20, 24, 79
absolute space, 21–23, 26, 30–31
adaptation, alliances and, 86–89
additive cumulation, 40–41
adversarial proximity, 114, 120, 122–127
Africa, 27, 52, 100
agent-structure framework, 5, 46, 154, 155
Agnew, John, 6, 17, 19, 25
air travel, 24–25
Aleprete, M. E., 161n4
aliens, 59
alliances, 15–16, 73–92, 158; borders and, 81; concept of, 74–77; decision to enter, 76–77, 91–92, 164n4; in geopolitics, 77–80; as instruments of adaptation, 86–89; opportunity and, 81–86; relative location and, 21; technology and, 87–89; war diffusion and, 81–82, 114–116; willingness and, 89–91
Anglophone countries, 27
Anselin, Luc, 17, 18, 35–37, 162n2, 163n10
anti-US alliances, 88–89
ARC/INFO, 98–99, 109
Armed Conflict Location and Event Dataset (ACLED), 97
artificial boundaries, 8
Austria, 147
authority, 2
Axtell, Robert, 162n4
Azar, Edward, 26

balance of power, 80
bandwagoning effect, 83
behavior, effect of space on, 28
Belgium, 139
blocs, 60–61
Bobrow, Davis, 2–3, 159
border disputes, 53–54
bordering process, 70–71
borderless world discourse, 69–70, 141
borders, 48, 52; alliances and, 81; colonial territories, 95, 114; conceptualizing, 93–97; conflict and, 49, 95, 113–136; in contemporary system, 64–65; contiguous, 28, 42–44, 48, 65–68, 82, 102, 114–127, 140–142; cooperation and, 137–152; creation of new, 44; critical boundaries and, 108–109; functions and consequences of, 68–71; GIS data on, 105–111, 113–114; globalization and, 57–72; homeland, 95, 114; importance of, 57–58, 71–72, 157–159; interaction across, 49–50; interaction opportunities and, 65–68, 94; interdependence/ integration and, 138–142; land, 66, 67; length of, 94, 117–119, 123–125; manipulable, 62; movement across, 67–68, 70; nature of, 105–109, 117–120, 125–126, 130–131, 134, 137–152; non-realist approaches to, 62–64; operationalization of, 96–97; pseudo-borders, 81; realist/legal notions of, 58–62; reconceptualizing, 113–136; salience, 14–15, 67, 102–105,

177

ecological triad, 6, 9–16, 73, 75–76, 154
economic interdependence, 63–64
economics, 6
Egypt, 62, 109
Elder, Charles, 129
elite powers, 158, 163n4
endowment effects, 55
enduring rivalries, 132–135
entity, 6, 9, 11
entity-environment relationship, 6, 9–16
environment, 6, 9, 10
environmental determinism, 4
environmental possibilism, 10
environmental probabilism, 10, 13, 155
Environmental Systems Research, Inc. (ESRI), 98
Epstein, Joshua, 162n4
ethnic-national groups, 27, 51
Euclidian space, 22
European Coal and Steel Community (ECSC), 140, 141
European Free Trade Area (EFTA), 147, 150
European Union, 44, 65, 70–71, 108, 121–122, 139–152
expected utility models, 55
exploratory spatial data analysis (ESDA), 37–38
externalities, 63

Fairgrieve, James, 85
fealty, 59
feudal model, 27, 58–59
First Law of Geography, 14
foreign policy: crisis, 120; determinist thinking and, 4; geography and, 7; substitutability, 74
Foucault, Michel, 7, 17–18, 21, 30
Fox, William T. R., 161n3
France, 139
Francophone countries, 27
Franco-Prussian relations, 161n1 (chap. 2)
free trade, 130
Friedman, Gil, 27, 54
Furlong, K., 97

Galton, Antony, 34–35
geographical information systems (GIS), 7, 28–29, 37, 93–111, 113, 156–157; ARC/INFO, 98–99; borders and, 105–111, 113–114; components of, 96; crisis analysis

using, 97, 122–127; to study cooperation, 137–138
geography: dynamism of, 153–159; as facilitating condition, 47–51; international relations and, 1–15, 153–159; new, 3–5, 9; political, 37, 79; as source of conflict, 51–55; stability of, 7
geopolitical context, 11–13; alliances within, 74–92; dynamic nature of, 7, 15–16; territoriality and, 60
geopolitics, 5, 7; alliances and, 73–92; deterministic, 24; dynamism of, 153–159; new, 62, 155; role of, 3
Geopolitik, 3
Germany, 44, 62, 89, 139
Gibler, Douglas, 97
Giddens, Anthony, 1–2, 12, 76, 79, 162n2
GIS. See geographical information systems (GIS)
Gleditsch, Kristian, 43, 97
globalization, borders and, 57–72, 157–159
Goertz, Gary, 118, 164n2 (chap. 5)
Goodchild, Michael F., 18, 163n10
Gray, Colin, 7, 80
Green, Elliott, 52
group identity, 32, 44–45, 51, 68–69
Gulf War, 26

Hammarstrom, Mats, 43
Haushofer school, 3
Heldt, Birger, 43
Herz, John, 60–61
hierarchical model, 27
Hoffman, A. A., 161n4
Holy Roman emperor, 59
homeland borders, 95, 114
hot spots, 97
Hug, Simon, 52
Huth, Paul, 52, 118

identity: group, 32, 44–45, 51, 68–69; national, 52; place and, 32, 44–45
ideology, 155
immigrants, 68
innovations, 14, 16
integration, 50, 63, 68, 127, 128–130, 138–142
integrative cumulation, 39–42
interaction opportunities, 42, 48–50, 65–68, 81–86, 94, 99–102, 131
interaction opportunity model, 13–16
intercontinental ballistic missiles (ICBMs), 25, 26, 87

About the Author

Harvey Starr is the Dag Hammarskjöld Professor in International Affairs in the Department of Political Science at the University of South Carolina. A leading authority on the study of conflict, geopolitics, and diffusion, Dr. Starr is author or coauthor of fourteen books and monographs and more than ninety journal articles and book chapters, including *World Politics: The Menu for Choice,* now in its tenth edition. He has served as president of the Conflict Processes Section of the APSA, as vice president of the APSA, as president of the Peace Science Society (International), and as vice president and president of the International Studies Association.